UNION INTERNATIONALE DES SCIENCES PRÉHISTORIQUES ET PROTOHISTORIQUES
INTERNATIONAL UNION OF PREHISTORIC AND PROTOHISTORIC SCIENCES

PROCEEDINGS OF THE XVI WORLD CONGRESS (FLORIANÓPOLIS, 4-10 SEPTEMBER 2011)
ACTES DU XVI CONGRÈS MONDIAL (FLORIANÓPOLIS, 4-10 SEPTEMBRE 2011)

(Session VII)

VOL. 5

Underwater Archaeology, Coastal and Lakeside

Edited by

Alexandra Figueiredo
Flavio Calippo
Gilson Rambelli

BAR International Series 2631
2014

Published in 2016 by
BAR Publishing, Oxford

BAR International Series 2631

Proceedings of the XVI world Congress of the International Union of Prehistoric and Protohistoric Sciences
Actes du XVI Congrès mondial de l'Union Internationale des Sciences Préhistoriques et Protohistoriques

Secretary of the Congress: Rossano Lopes Bastos
President of the Congress National Commission: Erika Robrhan-Gonzalez
Elected President: Jean Bourgeois
Elected Secretary General: Luiz Oosterbeek
Elected Treasurer: François Djindjian
Series Editors: Luiz Oosterbeek, Erika Robrhan-Gonzalez
Volume title: Underwater Archaeology, Coastal and Lakeside
Volume editors: Alexandra Figueiredo, Flavio Calippo, Gilson Rambelli

Underwater Archaeology, Coastal and Lakeside

ISBN 978 1 4073 1268 2

© The editors and contributors severally and the Publisher 2014

The signed papers are the sole responsibility of their authors.
Les textes signés sont de la seule responsabilité de leurs auteurs.

Contacts: General Secretariat of the U.I.S.P.P. – International Union of Prehistoric and
Protohistoric Sciences Instituto Politécnico de Tomar, Av. Dr. Cândido Madureira 13, 2300
TOMAR Email: uispp@ipt.pt

The authors' moral rights under the 1988 UK Copyright,
Designs and Patents Act are hereby expressly asserted.

All rights reserved. No part of this work may be copied, reproduced, stored,
sold, distributed, scanned, saved in any form of digital format or transmitted
in any form digitally, without the written permission of the Publisher.

BAR Publishing is the trading name of British Archaeological Reports (Oxford) Ltd.
British Archaeological Reports was first incorporated in 1974 to publish the BAR Series, International and
British. In 1992 Hadrian Books Ltd became part of the BAR group. This volume was originally published
by Archaeopress in conjunction with British Archaeological Reports (Oxford) Ltd / Hadrian Books Ltd,
the Series principal publisher, in 2014. This present volume is published by BAR Publishing, 2016.

Printed in England

BAR titles are available from:

	BAR Publishing
	122 Banbury Rd, Oxford, OX2 7BP, UK
EMAIL	info@barpublishing.com
PHONE	+44 (0)1865 310431
FAX	+44 (0)1865 316916
	www.barpublishing.com

Table of Contents

Table of Contents i
List of Figures and Tables ii
Preface v

ARCHAEOLOGY PRE AND PROTO-HISTORIC

UNDERWATER PREHISTORIC LANDSCAPE: PRELIMINARY RESULTS OF
    ARMAÇÃO DE PÊRA BAY 3
Leandro Infantini; Delminda Moura; Nuno Bicho

EVIDENCES AND HYPOTHESIS ABOUT THE ORIGIN AND USE OF NAUTICAL ARTIFACTS
    BETWEEN THE PEOPLE OF THE SAMBAQUIS (BRAZIL) 13
Flávio Rizzi Calippo

COASTLINE AND LITHIC TECHNOLOGY DURING THE TARDIGLACIAL IN THE ALGARVE 21
Carolina Mendonça; Leandro Infantini

LEGISLATION, METHODOLOGIES AND APPLIED SCIENCES

THE IMPORTANCE OF GIS IN UNDERWATER ARCHAEOLOGY 29
Alexandra Figueiredo; Isabel Bernardes

MUSEALIZATION OF THE UNDERWATER HERITAGE OF THE WATERS OF SERGIPE 33
Ângela Andrade Ferreira; Elizabete de Castro Mendonça

CAVE BACELINHO, ALVAIÁZERE – FROM SANTOS ROCHA TO THE NEW INVESTIGATIONS:
    THE CONSERVATION OF ARCHAEOLOGICAL IRON ARTEFACTS 39
Alexandra Figueiredo; Cláudio Monteiro; Helena Félix

MATERIAL PRESERVATION VS MATERIAL CONSERVATION: ANALYSIS AND
    CONSERVATION OF ARCHEOLOGICAL MATERIAL OF THE SITE SC-NAUF-01,
    SANTA CATARINA, BRAZIL 47
*Cláudio Monteiro; Deisi Scunderlick Eloy de Farias; Alexandra Figueiredo;
Maria Matilde Villegas Jaramillo*

THE STUDY AND ANALYSIS OF THE BEHAVIOUR OF WET ARCHAEOLOGICAL WOOD
    DURING THE DRYING PROCESS: THE DEVELOPMENT OF DRYING METHODS
    WITHOUT THE NEED OF CONSOLIDANTS OR PLASTICIZERS 55
Cláudio Monteiro

List of Figures and Tables

L. Infantini *et al.*: Underwater Prehistoric Landscape: Preliminary results of Armação de Pêra Bay

Figure 1 – Location of study area, using a Digital Elevation Model (DEM) to submerged area and panchromatic image (band 8) from Landsat7 satellite to continental area. Submerged area (DTM) was classified into ten groups of depth 4

Figure 2 – Left: Slope map with four classes (0-2%, 2-4%, 4-6% and >6%) and depth contours of -15, -18, -21, -24 e -26 meters 6

Figure 3 – Drainage network (black) created by numerical modelling using DTM, showing in dark grey the dry land (now submerged) when the mean sea level was at -19 m depth 7

Figure 4 – Underwater pictures, showing karsification evidences and sampling with drill system 7

Figure 5 – Map of Western Algarve showing depth contours of -15 and -120 m below MSL and archaeological site of Vale Boi. The low level (-120 m) correspond to the shoreline during the LGM, and the highest (-15 m) could be a shoreline during OIS3. In light grey, the continental shelf emerged during low sea levels, and in dark grey, the continent part 9

Table 1 – Depth of samples, percentage of carbonates and statistical analysis using Gradistat 5

Table 2 – Result of radiocarbon dating in a fragment of beach rock. Calibrated data was obtained using OxCal v4.1.7 with reservoir effect of 380 ± 30 5

F.R. Calippo: Evidences and hypothesis about the origin and use of nautical artifacts between the people...

Figure 1 – Representation of a *Kaveri* River fisherman (South India) using a float swimming 16

Figure 2 – Thumbnail of the raft of reeds found in northern Chile 17

Figure 3 – *Casa Santa* archaeological site, in *Carnaúba dos Dantas*, *Rio Grande do Norte*, Brazil 17

Figure 4 – Probable representation of a pirogue (classified as the *Nordeste* Tradition) in a rock shelter in *Seridó* region, in *Rio Grande do Norte*, Brazil 17

Figure 5 – Probable representation of a pirogue (classified as the *Nordeste* Tradition) in a rock shelter in *Seridó* region, in *Rio Grande do Norte*, Brazil 17

Figure 6 – Probable representation of a pirogue (classified as the *Nordeste* Tradition) in a rock shelter in *Seridó* region, in *Rio Grande do Norte*, Brazil 18

Figure 7 – Probable representation of a pirogue (classified as the *Nordeste* Tradition) in a rock shelter in *Seridó* region, in *Rio Grande do Norte*, Brazil..................................18

Figure 8 – Representation of dogout canoes found in the *Pedra do Alexandre* archaeological site, in *Carnauba dos Dantas*, *Rio Grande do Norte*, Brazil (c – representation of a canoe that carries seven people led by a chief who sports long feather headdress; g: probable representation of a sail) 18

C. Mendonça & L. Infantini: Coastline and lithic technology during the Tardiglacial in the Algarve

Figure 1 – Digital Terrain Model (MDT), with altimetric and bathymetric data of the Algarve, and archaeological sites in the area..22

Figure 2 – Evolution of sea level in the portuguese continental shelf, covering last 20 ky BP, with Magdalenian chronologies..23

Figure 3 – Location sites of *Praia da Galé* and *Lagoa do Bordoal* and an indication of (likely) coastline to the Middle Magdalenian (-100 meters deep), demonstrating the vast territory emerged in the period 23

Figure 4 – Location of sites *Vale Boi, Vale Santo 4, Ponta Garcia* and *Praia de Albandeira*, with their distances from the (probably) coastline between -100 m to -30 meters depth, showing the variation of the area emerged and submerged during the period 24

A. Figueiredo *et al.*: Cave Bacelinho, Alvaiázere – from Santos Rocha to the new investigations...

Figure 1 – General plan of the cave showing the entrance area of the cavity, enclosed rooms and galleries 40

Figure 2 – The room layout with the detail of the stone structures, concentrating zone coals (squares B and C) and fireplace (grid A1)..............................41

Figure 3 – Excavated area with the spatial representation of the elements of glass, metal and lithic 41

Figure 4 – Drawing (a) and photo of Lucerne (b) (II and III century AD).........................42

Figure 5 – The room layout indicating the squares and metal artifacts recovered 42

Figure 6 – Detail of sword treated, which is visible the uneven caused by the increase of metal 43

Figure 7 – Wedge, after clean, where you can observe the deformation and small superficial blisters 43

Figure 8 – Arrowhead, after clean, where we can observe the small superficial blisters..43

Figure 9 – Sword, in iron, double-edged, before (A) and after (B) the conservation treatment, from the raster C2, level 2 44

Figure 10 – Sword, in iron, before (A) and after (B) treatment of conservation, from raster C3, level 2 44

Figure 11 – Buckle, in iron, before (A) and after (B) the conservation treatment, coming from the raster B3, level 2 44

Figure 12 – Nozzle arms, in iron, before (A) and after (B) the intervention. We can verify the amount of concretions and encrustations before the intervention 44

C. Monteiro *et al.*: Material preservation vs material conservation...

Figure 1 – Location of the archaeological site where treated materials were exhumed 48

Figure 2 – Process of desalination 50

Figure 3 – a and b – Blazon of Lion and Castile with Portuguese symbol indicating the period of Iberian Union (1580-1640). We can easily observe two lions, one in the inferior right side and another in superior side and two towers on opposite corners of lions. They are crowned at the top. We can observe five Portuguese chines 50

Figure 4 – Stone in triangular shape with bas-relief in Latin where we can read "*PHILIPPVS MAXIMVS CATHOLICVS II HISPANIARVM INDIARVM ET REX ANNO 158.2*" It is an allusion to King Phillip II 51

Figure 5 – Example of one of the spheres, possibly to compound an adornments architectonic work. There is a pyramidal engaging hole that is long-drawn until 1/3 of the piece 51

Figure 6 – The X-Ray allowed identify a fragment of a small iron rod of rectangular hollow section that possibly could be twisted by a rope, visible by traces of empty spaces left on the concretions 52

Frame 1 – Categories of artefacts identified in SC-NAUF-01 49

Frame 2 – Description of stonework pieces 51

C. Monteiro: The study and analysis of the behaviour of wet archaeological wood during the drying process

Figure 1 – Drying program in sample A2 57

Figure 2 – Wood before treatment 57

Figure 3 – Wood after treatment 57

Figure 4 – A1 Before 58

Figure 5 – A1 After 58

Figure 6 – A2 Before 58

Figure 7 – A2 After 58

Figure 8 – A1 After being dried 40x 58

Figure 9 – A2 After being dried 40x 58

Figure 10 – B1 Before starting process 59

Figure 11 – B1 During process 59

Figure 12 – B1 Final Phase of process 59

Figure 13 – B2 Before starting process 59

Figure 14 – B2 During process 59

Figure 15 – B2 Final Phase of process 59

Preface

This book presents a collection of peer-reviewed papers from the sixteenth UISPP / SAB, session VII, titled **Underwater Archaeology, Coastal and Lakeside**, held in the Federal University of Santa Catarina (UFSC), Campus Trindade, Florianópolis / SC – Brazil, in September 2011.

The UISPP conference, founded on May 28, 1931, had for the first time a session related to underwater archaeology, applied by Comission IV, and we had the pleasure to coordinate it. In the session were presented several papers and related posters some of which are now brought together in this book.

Our main objective for the session was to organize it such a manner that it encouraged interaction between the different projects and between senior leading scientists and young researchers.

Underwater Archaeology has made great strides in the study of pre and proto-historic societies. Its importance is beginning to be reflected in the scientific community which is looking for new forms and data about the human past.

We intended to:

– promote the study, preservation and discussion of wet or submerged archaeological sites

– provide co-existence, dialogue and relationships between researchers, students and personalities linked to various areas under discussion

– provide the ideal opportunity for exchanging ideas, experiences and new findings on the application of underwater archeology to the study of the human past

Whereas this technical and methodological discipline is still young, we chose to open the session to all historical periods. It was also worth considering the importance of the relationship that archaeologists engaged in with the auxiliary sciences during the study of wet or waterlogged archaeological sites. We divided the session into three different themes: Archaeology Pre and Proto-Historic, Historical Archaeology and Legislation, Methodologies and Applied Sciences. We had received about 15 paper submissions. Of the papers and posters presented associated with the theme and sent to be part of the proceedings, we have used eight, that follow in this book.

Finally, we would like to acknowledge and thank everyone who made the production of the congress, session and this book possible.

The Editors
Alexandra Figueiredo
Gilson Rambelli
Flavio Calippo

ARCHAEOLOGY PRE AND PROTO-HISTORIC

UNDERWATER PREHISTORIC LANDSCAPE: PRELIMINARY RESULTS OF ARMAÇÃO DE PÊRA BAY

Leandro INFANTINI & Nuno BICHO
UNIARQ – Centro de Arqueologia da Universidade de Lisboa

Delminda MOURA
CIMA (Centro de Investigação Marinha e Ambiental) – Universidade do Algarve

Abstract: *During the Last Glacial Maximum (LGM) wide portions of the continental shelves were emerged due to a wide marine regression. Accordingly, the landscape and therefore prehistoric heritage and palaeoenvironmental indicators are currently submerged and potentially preserved, being necessary investigations in order to study and restore this heritage. Aiming to contribute for the understanding of underwater landscape, this work presents preliminary data on research in the submerged area of the Armação de Pêra bay (Southern Portugal). However, due to difficulties of working in underwater areas, from the morphological characterization to sampling for textural analysis, new approaches were needed to investigate this area. Characterization and morphological analysis of the study area were performed in GIS environment using a Digital Elevation Model (DEM). Based on this analysis, the submerged area of the Bay of Armação de Pêra shows morphology compatible with the development of a coastal lagoon system during the Pleistocene, sheltered by a spitbar. As observed in preliminary petrographic and sedimentological analysis carried out on sample taken from diving, the sands of the sedimentary body have suffered a rapid cementation by calcium carbonate that gave them strength to erosion by waves and currents.*

Keywords: *GIS, Digital Elevation Model, Morphology, Coastline, Prehistory*

Résumé: *Pendant le Dernier Maximum Glaciaire (DMG) de grandes portions de plateau continental ont été émergé en raison de la régression marine de grande amplitude. Ainsi, une grande partie du paysage et, par conséquent le patrimoine préhistorique et paléoenvironnementales est actuellement submergé et potentiellement préservés, étant enquêtes nécessaires en vue d'étudier et de récupérer ce patrimoine. Dans ce contexte, et de contribuer à la connaissance des paysages submergés, dans le objectiv de cet article est de présenter et de discuter des données préliminaires des recherches effectuées dans la zone submergée de la baie de Armação de Pêra (sud du Portugal). Toutefois, en raison de difficultés inhérentes à travailler dans les zones submergées, de la caractérisation morphologique des échantillons pour analyse de texture, de nouvelles approches méthodologiques ont été nécessaires pour caractériser la zone d'étude. Caractérisation et l'analyse morphologique de la zone d'étude a été réalisée dans un environnement SIG en utilisant un Modèle Numérique d'Elévation (MNE) de la région. Sur la base de cette analyse, la zone submergée de la baie de Armação de Pera présente une morphologie compatible avec le développement d'un système lagunaire au cours du Pléistocène, à l'abri d'un banc de sable. Comme l'a observé dans les analyses préliminaires pétrographiques et sédimentologiques, effectuée sur des échantillons prélevés à partir de la plongée, les sables de la barre a subi une rapide cimentation de carbonate de calcium qui leur a donné la force de l'érosion par les vagues et les courants.*

Mots-clés: *SIG, Modèle Numérique d'Elévation, Morphologique, ligne de côte, Préhistorique*

1. INTRODUCTION

Sea level changes and climate changes were the natural phenomena with major impact on environmental evolution during the Quaternary. The expansion of ice caps and continental glaciers during Pleistocene glaciations caused the decreasing in the volume of ocean water causing the lowering of mean sea level. In opposition, during the warmer periods, partial melting of glaciers induced a rise in mean sea level (e.g. Ponzi, 2004).

In this context, the sea level changes have impact on the inhabitants of susceptible areas because of the exposure or flooding of parts of this territory, altering the dynamic relationship between the exploitation of natural resources, especially marine resources. Furthermore, the coastline has a great ecological importance because it is the boundary between terrestrial and marine environments, and human communities adapt to this dynamic. In this sense, it is very important to the question the identification of paleoshorelines to identify the sea level, the spatial distribution of archaeological sites and to relationship of the exploitation of marine resources

Changes in the coastline over the past resulted in erosion processes, transport and deposition. Several evidence of ancient coastlines, such as coastal platforms, cliffs and slope ruptures, can be identified using remote sensing systems (Bird, 2008). Following the analysis of the bathymetry carried out within this work and the descripttions by Vanney & Mougenot (1981) who reported a underwater Plio-Pleistocene relief, parallel to the coastline, this study aims to investigate the submerged area of the Armação de Pêra Bay, since this area provides a morphology consistent with the development of a spitbar protecting a coastal lagoon, which in the past should be of great importance as a food source.

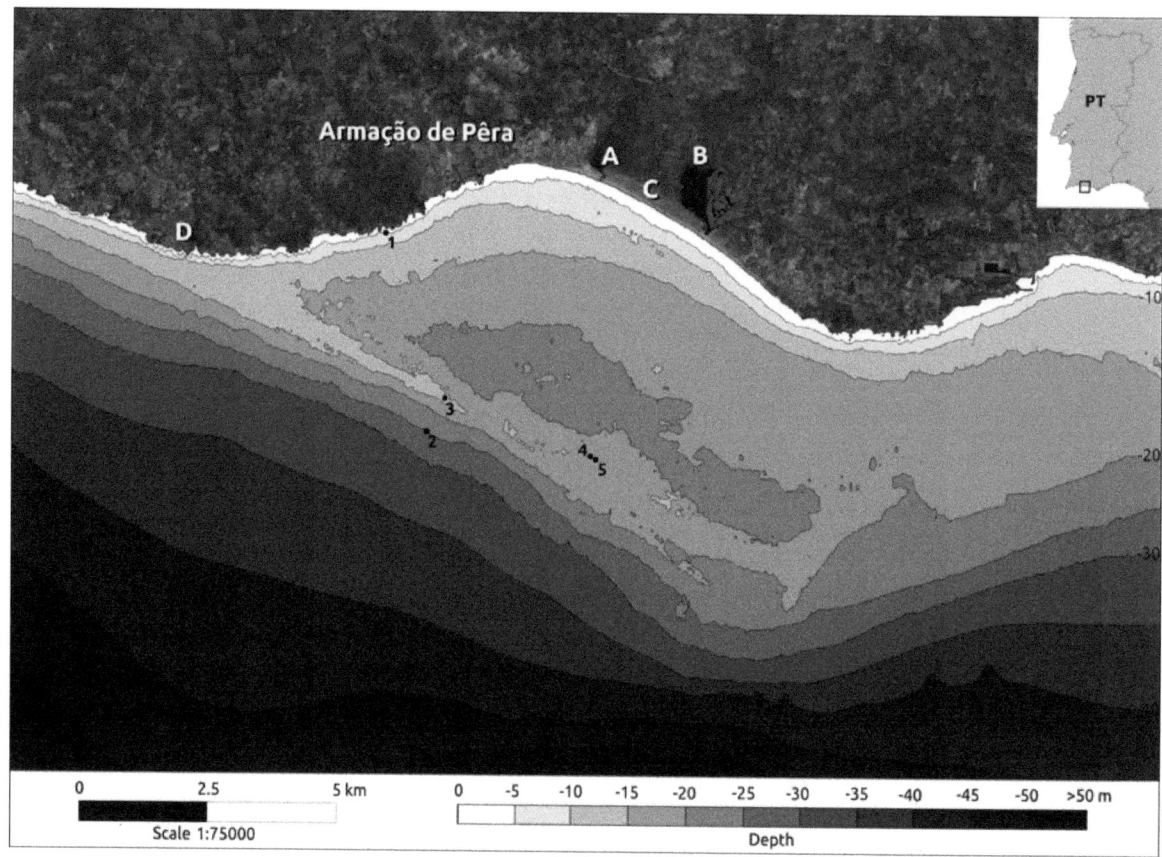

Figure 1 – Location of study area, using a Digital Elevation Model (DEM) to submerged area and panchromatic image (band 8) from Landsat7 satellite to continental area. Submerged area (DTM) was classified into ten groups of depth. Location of samples: A – Alcantarilha estuary; B – Espiche estuary; C – Dune field; D – Cape Carvoeiro; 1 – Samples AL-01 e AL-02; 2 – Samples PT-1F e PT-1S; 3 – Samples PT-2B; 4 – Samples PC-SP e PC-SL; 5 – Samples AP-01

A spitbar can be defined as a type of barrier, formed along the down-drift longshore by the accumulation of sediments and mainly shaped by waves and currents (Davis Jr. & Fitzgerald, 2004; Bird, 2008). The genesis of a spitbar occurs when flux energy and consequent transport efficacy decreases due to factors such as morphology or changes in the coastline direction, allowing the deposition of sediment. Some spitbar are curved due to deposition of sediment at the end of the bar adjacently to a river mouth, and may indicate either the position of the coastline and the evolution of the sandbank itself (Ciavola, 1997; Davis Jr. & Fitzgerald, 2004; Jewell, 2007; Lindhorst et al., 2008).These barrier systems can protect the bays, coastal lagoons and marshes, that are habitats of great importance for the breeding of marine organisms and a major source of nutrients (Davis & Fitzgerald, Jr., 2004). Thus, the identification of these paleoenvironments, in addition of providing an indicator of the evolution of the coastline, currents and wave direction, may contribute to the understanding of the exploitation of aquatic resources for the diet of prehistoric human communities.

2. CARACTERIZATION OF AREA

The Armação de Pêra Bay (Fig. 1) is located in the Algarve region, southern Portugal. It is a zeta-form bay, where a beach of 6 km length is interrupted only by the Alcantarilha and Espiche estuaries. The beach is landward limited by a dune field that reaches 200-300 meters wide that overlies a paleodune system. This paleodune field together with the occurrence of beachrock, point to the mean sea level stabilization *circa* 5000 years (Moura et al., 2007; Teixeira, 1999).

A NW-SE calcarenite ridge 1 km wide occurs between -14 and -25 m deep at the Armação de Pêra Bay. Its age not yet well constrained may be addressed to the Late Pleistocene (Teixeira 1999; Teixeira & Pinto, 2002).

The Algarve coast has a mesotidal regime, ranging between 1.3 and 3.5 m at neap and spring tides respectively. The waves approach the shore mainly from WSW (72% of occurrences) being the significant height less than 1 m rarely exceeding 3 m (2% of annual occurrence) during storms (Costa et al., 2001).

3. MATERIALS AND METHODS

Due to logistical difficulties of this research, it was necessary a development of two main approaches. On one hand, was necessary to collect samples in a underwater context to textural analysis and dating; on the other hand, was necessary the development and management of a

Geographic Information System (GIS) for the characterization, morphological analysis and for the planning a sampling campaigns.

3.1 Morphological Analysis

The study area was identified and selected due to the potential preservation of the paleocoastline by a Geographic Information System (GIS), using a Digital Elevation Model (DEM) and among others geo-referenced information (Infantini, 2012).

GIS can be defined as the geo-processing and computational tools that allow complex analysis, by integration of multiple data sources and the creation of geo-referenced databases (Câmara et al., 2001). In this context, the GIS use data from multiple sources, such as DEM developed by Luis (2010) using altimetric and bathymetric data with 50 meters of spatial resolution, DEM data from Shuttle Radar Topography Mission (Jarvis et al., 2008) with 90 meters of spatial resolution, and Landsat7 satellite imagery with 30 meters of spatial resolution. This work used several free access computational tools (Open Source), as the GNU/Linux Ubuntu 11.04 operating system and the softwares Quantum GIS 1.7.3 (Quantum GIS Development Team, 2011), SPRING 5.1.8 (Câmara et al., 1996), and Mirone 2.1.1 (Luis, 2007).

Based on GIS, several operations were carried out from the Digital Elevation Model (DEM), including the calculation of slopes, builduing of the drainage network system and planning a location of underwater samplings. The slopes were reclassified into four classes (0 to 2%, 2 to 4%, 4 to 6% and more than 6%) in order to identify the main groups of breaks of slope and coastal platforms. The drainage network of emerged and submerged areas was represented through a hydrologic model of flow based on the DEM, integrating altimetry and bathymetry.

3.2 Sampling

Several dives took place for the collection of samples in the area aiming lithologycal identification and characterization. In these dives, in addition to surface samples, some samples were collected using an underwater drilling system. This system is autonomous, since it uses the air pressure from a secondary air cylinder and was developed to take samples with less biogenic activity than surface samples. The principle is the same of SCUBA diving system, using a pressure regulator (first stage) for reducing the air pressure from cylinder to an intermediate pressure to the use in a drilling system. In this sampling system we used a pneumatic drill and a core drill with 30 mm of diameter.

Sampling locations were selected previously from GIS and bathymetric DEM. A total of eight samples were selected for textural analysis and radiocarbon dating (Tables 1 and 2).

3.3 Textural Analysis

The seven samples (Table 1) were treated with H_2O_2 (110 v.) to cleaning marine organisms. Subsequently, they were immersed in a solution of HCl (20%) to determine the total of calcium carbonate (by difference in weight before and after dissolution by acid). The resulting detrital fractions were sieved mechanically by a set of sieves of mesh range ½ Φ. The statistical analysis was performed by *Gradistat* (Blott, 2010). Another sample (Table 2) was dated by University of Waikato radiocarbon lab, New Zealand.

Table 1 – Depth of samples, percentage of carbonates and statistical analysis (Folk e Ward method) using Gradistat (Blott, 2010)

Samples	Depth m	CaCO3 %	Mean Φ unit	Sorting σ	Skewness *Sk*	Kurtosis *K*
AL-01	-7	80,70	2,78 Fine sand	0,75 Moderately sorted	-0,36 Very coarse skewed	1,59 Very leptokurtic
AL-02	-7	76,11	2,55 Fine sand	0,92 Moderately sorted	-0,36 Very coarse skewed	1,14 Leptokurtic
PT-2B	-15	61,35	2,45 Fine sand	0,52 Moderately well sorted	-0,26 Coarse skewed	1,38 Leptokurtic
PC-SP	-18	63,03	1,84 Medium sand	0,81 Moderately sorted	-0,26 Coarse skewed	0,70 Platykurtic
PC-SL	-18	47,09	1,15 Medium sand	0,69 Moderately well sorted	0,71 Very fine skewed	2,75 Very leptokurtic
PT-1F	-25	60,16	1,19 Medium sand	0,64 Moderately well sorted	0,60 Very fine skewed	0,82 Platykurtic
PT-1S	-25	63,18	2,08 Fine sand	0,89 Moderately sorted	-0,35 Very coarse skewed	0,83 Platykurtic

Table 2 – Result of radiocarbon dating in a fragment of beach rock. Calibrated data was obtained using OxCal v4.1.7 (Bronk Ramsey, 2001) with reservoir effect of 380 ± 30 (Soares, 1993)

Sample	Code	Depth. (m)	Material	Method	Result (BP)	*cal* BP (1σ)
AP-01	Wk-30540	-18	Cement ($CaCO_3$)	AMS	17,581 ± 56	20,145 – 19,618

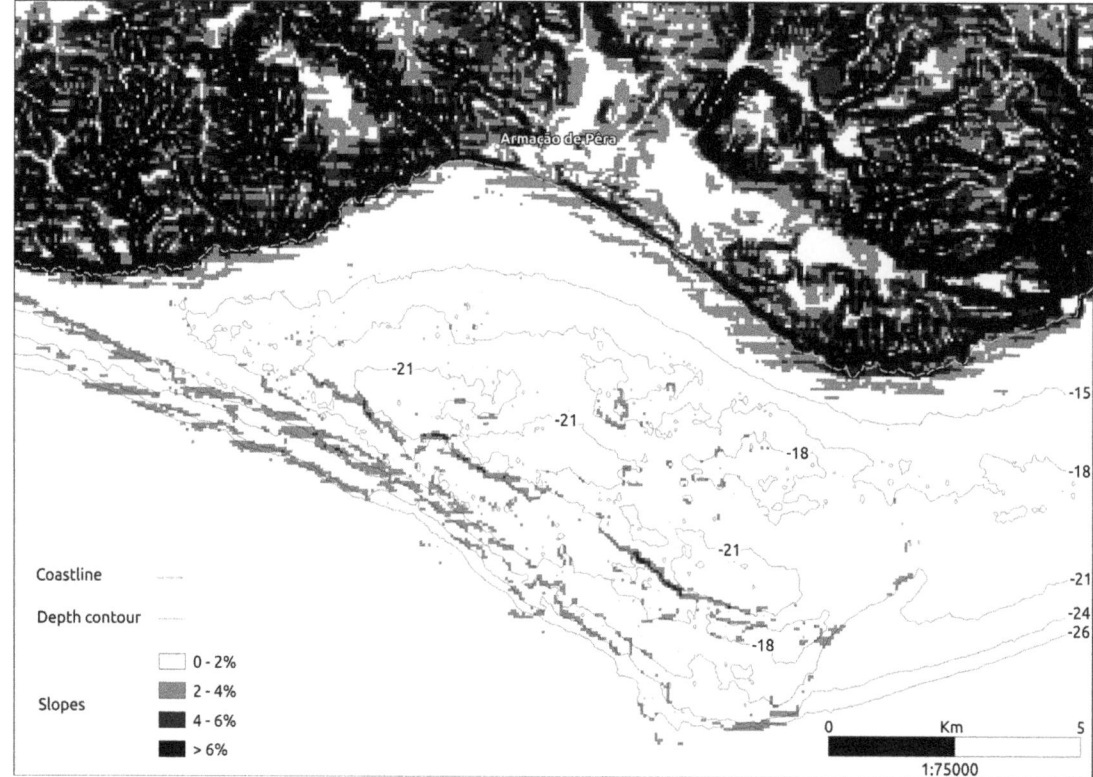

Figure 2 – Left: Slope map with four classes (0-2%, 2-4%, 4-6% and >6%) and depth contours of -15, -18, -21, -24 e -26 meters

4. RESULTS

4.1 Morphology

The underwater sedimentary relief is, approximately, parallel to coastline (Armação de Pêra beach) and have physiographic features consistent with a paleo spitbar (later cemented) build approximately from Carvoeiro Cape, where it is anchored (Fig. 1).

The submerged area is mostly comprised by categories of slope between 0-2%, a common gradient in continental shelf (Fig. 2). However, slopes between 2% to 4% are associated with depths -15, -18, -21, -24 and -26 m suggesting that these slopes can be carved by sea during sea level changes after cementation.

Possible paleochanels of the drainage network was detected the in the submerged area (Fig. 3), probably carved when sea level was lower than the present. Still, in diving, we observed several karstic forms (Fig. 4).

4.2 Textural Analysis

The percentage of total calcium carbonate of the samples range between 47% to 80% (Table 1). The higher carbonate content is AL-01 and AL-02, located in the Albandeira beach into -7 m depth (Fig. 1 and Table 1). The mean of grains range from 1.14 to 2.78 Φ, between fine sand to medium sand and ranging from moderately to moderately well sorted (Table 1). The Skewness is between 0.7 and -3.6.

Morphoscopic analysis was performed on quartz grains in the size fractions 0.500, 0.355 and 0.250 mm. Samples PT-1F, PT-1S, PT-2B, PC-SP and PC-SL (Table 1) is mostly hyaline quartz with precipitation of iron oxide on the surface. The quartz grains are sub-angular to very angular. Following ultrasonic cleaning, the grains showed bright with frequent dissolution and impact marks. Samples Al-01 and AL-02 (Table 1) are composed by fine gray sand with occasional pyrite and abundant worms tubes constructed with detrital sediment.

4.3 Dating

The sample AP-01 was dated by radiocarbon indicating a rock cement formation of 17,581 ± 56 BP (Table 2). However, this dating must be interpreted with caution, since there are several problems associated with the dating this context, such as contamination by biogenic activity.

5. DISCUSSION

5.1 Morphology

The spitbar results from the accretion of underwater sediments in below base of waves and are often in down-drift of river mouths (Ciavola 1997, Simms *et al.*, 2006; Costas & Fitzgerald, 2011). The cape Carvoeiro is a natural obstacle to longshore drift, predominantly from West direction (Dias, 1988), and the decreasing of transport efficacy resulted in the accumulation of a

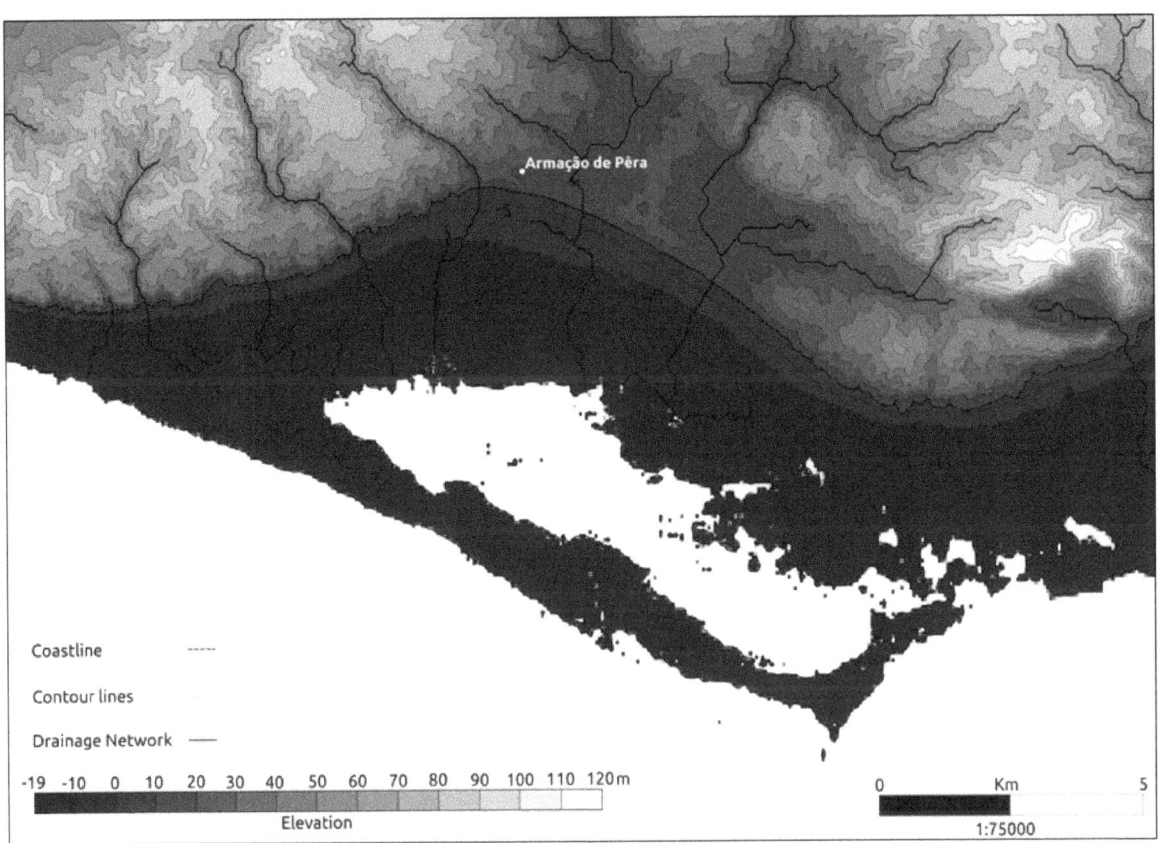

Figure 3 – Drainage network (black) created by numerical modelling using DTM, showing in dark grey the dry land (now submerged) when the mean sea level was at -19 m depth

Figure 4 – Underwater pictures, showing karsification evidences and sampling with drill system

spitbar until, approximately, the paleoestuaries of Alcantarilha and Espiche (Fig. 1 and 3). The result was a development spitbar characterized in the morphology.

The slopes associated with -15, -18, -21, -24 and -26 m depth (Fig. 2) were probably carved by sea level changes after the consolidation of this relief, since the difference between the depths (3 m) corresponds approximately to the tidal regime of Algarve. The slopes in the inner barrier are associated with the depth of -18 m were probably formed during direct exposure to the sea, because at -19 m this inner zone were closed forming a coastal lagoon (Fig. 3).

5.2 Sedimentological characteristics

Skewness less than 0.1, such as samples PT-1S; PT-2B; PC-SP, are typical beach sediments (Tanner, 1995), and skewness greater than 0.1 (samples PT-1F and PC-SL) are characteristic of marine restricted basins or aeolian sediments (Tanner, 1995). However, the impact and dissolution marks identified in morphoscopy, are characteristic of high energy aquatic environments (Azevedo, 1983). The standard deviation between 0.3 to 0.5 is characteristic of mature beaches, worked by length waves, but none of the samples are under these conditions. In fact, the quartz grains mainly sub-angular to very angular are more compatible with the rapid deposition from a decelerating flow than a successive transport by waves. According to Allen (1965) and Fleming (1977) mean grain size between 2.3 and 3.2 Φ are associated with sediment deposition of a flow velocity slows down to less than 24 cm/s^{-1}.

According to the previously expressed, samples PT-2B, PC-SP, PT-1S, PT-1F and PC-SL (Table 1) collected between -25 to -15 depth, are compatible with deposition in sandbar. The carbonate cement grain small and non equigranular is compatible with rapid cementation in sub-air environment.

However, samples AL-01 and AL-02, collected in -7 m depth, were deposited in an complete different environment. It is a gray fine sand with preserved abundant polychaetes tubes constructed with agglutinated sediment. They are common in intertidal coastal plains where they live in colonies (Fournier et al., 2010).

5.3 Paleoenvironment evolution

One hypothesis is that the formation of this barrier system occurred during OIS3 (Oxygen Isotope Stage), probably between 25 ky and 30 ky. Gracia indicates that between 20-30 ky sea level would be no less than -30 m depth today in the Cadiz Gulf (Gracia et al., 2008). Dabrio also indicates a high sea level between 25-30 ky to the Spanish southwest in the area of Cadiz to Huelva (Dabrio et al., 2000). In addition, the sedimentary fill of the Guadiana river estuary indicates that first estuarine sediments, prior to ca. 17 ky BP, are probably OIS3 or OIS5 (Boski et al., 2002). Moreover, in the U.S. Atlantic coast, there are formations associated with *middle Wisconsin* (OIS3), showing also a highstand (-15 m) of sea level (Rodriguez et al., 2000).

Finally, the spitbar was cemented by calcium carbonate and karstified by sub-air erosion. During the Last Glacial Maximum (LGM) the continental shelf was exposed and cementing and karstification must be occurred during this period, which point a genesis of sandbar in climatic event before LGM. The age of 17,581 BP obtained for carbonate cement is probably sub estimated, which can be explained by contamination of the sample by biogenic activity. Accordingly, it is necessary to invest in new campaigns to collect a large number of samples for dating, characterization and textural analysis.

5.4 Archaeological Context

The above hypothesis could explain the exploration of marine resources in archaeological sites, especially in Vale Boi, site located in Southern Portugal, as previously argued by Bicho (2004). Vale Boi is located little more 2 km away from the present coastline, on a slope of open river valley area, and is characterized by different exploittation of marine resources during Prehistory. The site consists of a long chronological sequence, including the entire Upper Palaeolithic since early Gravettian to late Magdalenian (Bicho & Haws, 2007; Bicho & Haws 2008).

In the Gravettian levels of Vale Boi, dated to ca. 33-24 kyr *cal* BP (Bicho et al, in press), there is an intensive use of different marine resources. This use decreased during the Solutrean, near the Last Glacial Maximum (LGM – ca. 18 kyr BP), increasing only in Mesolithic, ca. 9 kyr (Bicho & Haws, 2007, Bicho & Haws 2008).

In this sense, a sea high level can indicate that the use of marine resources, among other issues, could be related to the distance between the archaeological site and the coastline. During the Gravettian chronology, sea level could be higher and coastline should still be close enough to the intensive exploitation of these resources, declining in the later stages because the lowering of the ocean and increasing the distance of archaeological site to coastline due to Last Glacial Maximum (LGM).

Using GIS and the DEM to simulate a mean sea level during Gravettian on -15 m depth (highest sample collected), the shoreline would be around 1 km from the actually shoreline due to submarine morphology of the area near Vale Boi site (Fig. 5). Thus, applying the hypothesis discussed about high sea level during 25-30 kyr, the shoreline could be 3,5 km away from the site of Vale Boi during Gravettian. In other hand, during the Solutrean (LGM), and according of sea level curve of Portugal (Dias et al., 2000), the mean sea level was around -120 m below present and the shoreline was around 21 Km from Vale Boi site.

Thus, we could have had important changes in the coastlines and the paleoenvironment during the Upper Paleolithic. In fact, during the LGM, a large portion of continental shelf was emerged and probably occupied by hunter-garters communities. In this way,

6. CONCLUSION

The Geographic Information Systems (GIS) are an extremely important tool for paleoenvironmental

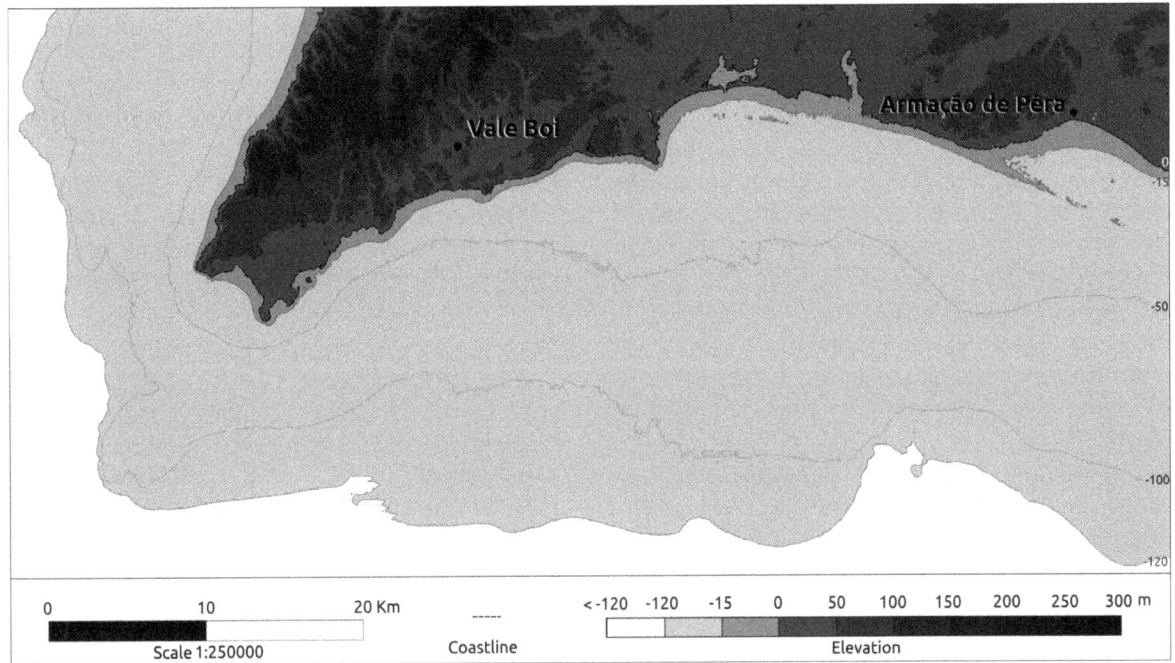

Figure 5 – Map of Western Algarve showing depth contours of -15 and -120 m below MSL and archaeological site of Vale Boi. The low level (-120 m) correspond to the shoreline during the LGM, and the highest (-15 m) could be a shoreline during OIS3. In light grey, the continental shelf emerged during low sea levels, and in dark grey, the continent part

research, allowing detection of morphologies of interest for investigation, as slope breaks and platforms, as well as to identify paleochannels of the drainage system.

This research was carried out mainly on a Digital Elevation Model (DEM). In this sense, is very important, to reveal more details of the area, build a elevation model with higher spatial resolution, especially bathymetry, through the using of remote sensing systems. Also, more dives and collecting samples are needed, both for the characterization of the rocks and for radiocarbon dating.

Nevertheless, preliminary data presented here, based on the morphology and textural analysis, indicates a formation an spitbar in Armação de Pêra bay before the Last Glacial Maximum (LGM). The various evidences presented, it seems reasonable to suppose that the formation of this system during OIS3, maybe between 25 to 30 kyr, with sea level between -25 m to -15 m depth (samples collected).

Thus, taking into account the data and findings presented here, the Armação de Pêra bay have great potential for paleoenvironmental reconstructions, especially about the sea level and coastline, and its great importance to the relationship with archaeology during the prehistory, requiring more investigation in this area.

Acknowledgements

This work is part of the research projects "Coastline evolution of the Algarve under a archaeological perspective" (SFRH/BD/47538/2008) and "The last Neanderthals and the emergence of Modern Humans in Southwestern Iberia" (PTDC/HIS-ARQ/117540/2010), funded by the for Science and Technology Foundation (FCT), Portugal.

Thanks to Miguel Rodrigues (Divespot Ltd) and Pedro Neves (Diving Center, University of Algarve) by some samples and underwater images, to Joaquim Luis (UAlg) by DEM, and the projects PTDC/CTE-GIX/111230/2009 (EROS) and SPLASHCOS (Submerged Prehistoric Archaeology and Landscapes of the Continental Shelf) – COST Action TD0902.

References

ALLEN, J.R.L. (1965) – A review of the origin and characteristics of recent alluvial sediments. Sedimentology, 5, 89-191.

AZEVEDO, M.T.M. (1983) – Exoscopia. Textos e Documentos de Apoio ao Ensino, Departamento de Geologia, Faculdade de Ciências, Universidade de Lisboa, 24 p.

BICHO, N. (2004) – As comunidades humanas de caçadores-recolectores do Algarve Ocidental: Perspectiva Arqueológica. In: Cardoso, L.C., Tavares, A.A. & Tavares, M.J.F. *Evolução Geohistórica do litoral português e fenómenos correlativos: Geologia, História, Arqueologia e Climatologia*, Lisboa: Europress. pp. 359-396.

BICHO, N.F.; HAWS, J. (2007) – Sea level changes and the impact on Late Pleistocene and Early Holocene Portuguese Prehistory. In: Bicho, N. From the Mediterran basin to the Portuguese Atlantic shore:

Paper in Honor of Anthony Marks, Actas IV congresso de arqueologia peninsular. Promontoria monográfica 07, Universidade do Algarve. pp. 37-56.

BICHO, N.F.; HAWS, J. (2008) – At the land's end: Marine resources and the importance of fluctuations in the coastline in the prehistoric hunter–gatherer economy of Portugal. Quaternary Science Reviews, Volume 27, issues 23-24, pp. 2166-2175.

BICHO, N.F.; HAWS, J.; MARREIROS, J., (no prelo) – Desde el Mondego al Guadiana: la ocupación Gravetiense de la fachada atlántica portuguesa. Actas do congreso El Gravetiense Cantábrico. Museo de Altamira.

BIRD, E. (2008) – Coastal Geomorphology: an introduction. Second Edition, Wiley ed., Chichester.

BRONK RAMSEY, C. (2001) – Development of the radiocarbon calibration program OxCal. Radiocarbon, 43(2A), p. 355-363.

BLOTT, S. (2010) – GRADISTAT: A Grain Size Distribution and Statistics Package for the Analysis of Unconsolidated Sediments by Sieving or Laser Granulometer (v. 4.0).

BOSKI, T.; MOURA, D.; VEIGA-PIRES, C.; CAMACHO, S.; DUARTE, D.; SCOTT, D.; FERNANDES, S.G. (2002) – Postglacial sea-level rise and sedimentary response in the Guadiana Estuary, Portugal/Spain border. Sedimentary Geology, 150, pp. 103-122.

CÂMARA, G.; DAVIS, C.; MONTEIRO, A.M.V. (2001) – Introdução à Ciência da Geoinformação. São josé dos Campos, DPI/INPE.

CÂMARA, G.; SOUZA, R.C.M.; FREITAS, U.M.; GARRIDO, J. (1996) – SPRING: Integrating remote sensing and GIS by object-oriented data modelling. Computers & Graphics, 20: (3), pp. 395-403.

CIAVOLA, P. (1997) – Coastal dynamics and impact of coastal protection works on the Spurn Head spit (UK). Catena, 30, 369-389.

COSTA, M.; SILVA, R. & VITORINO, J. (2001) – Contribuição para o estudo do clima de agitação marítima na costa portuguesa. 2a Jornadas Portuguesas de Engenharia Costeira e Portuária. Associação Nacional de Navegação. Sines, 20p.

COSTAS, S.; FITZGERALD, D. (2011) – Sedimentary architecture os a spit-end (Salisbury Beach, Massachusetts): The imprints of sea-level rise and inlet dynamics. Marine Geology, 284, 203-216.

DABRIO, C.J.; ZAZO, C.; GOY, J.L.; SIERRO, F.J.; BORJA, F.; LARIO, J.; GONZALES, J.A.; FLORES, J.A. (2000) – Depositional history of estuary infill during the last postglacial transgression (Gulf of Cadiz, Southern Spain). Marine Geology 162, 381–404.

DAVIS, JR, R. & FITZGERALD, D., (2008) – Beachs and coasts. Blackwell publishing, Oxford.

DIAS, J.M.A. (1988) – Aspectos geológicos do Litoral Algarvio. Geonovas, Vol. 10, Lisboa, p. 113-128.

DIAS, J.M.A.; BOSKI, T.; RODRIGUES, A.; MAGALHÃES, F. (2000) – Coast line Evolution in Portugal since the Last Glacial Maximum until Present – A Synthesis. Marine Geology, 170:177-186.

FOURNIER, J.; ETIENNE, S.; LE CAM, J.B. (2010) – Inter- and intraspecific variability in the chemical composition of the mineral phase of cements from several tube-building polychaetes. Geobios 43, p. 191-200.

GRACIA, F.J.; RODRÍGUEZ-VIDAL, J.; CÁCERES, L.M.; BELLUOMINI, G.; BENAVENTE, J.; ALONSO, C. (2008) – Diapiric uplift of an MIS 3 marine deposit in SW Spain: Implications for Late Pleistocene sea level reconstruction and palaeogeography of the Strait of Gibraltar. Quaternary Science Reviews, Volume 27, issues 23-24.

INFANTINI, L.R. (2012) – Paisagem Pré-histórica submersa da Baía de Armação de Pêra. MA thesis, University of Algarve.

JARVIS, A.; REUTER, H.I.; NELSON, A.; GUEVARA, E. (2008) – Hole-filled SRTM for the globe Version 4, available from the CGIAR-CSI SRTM 90 m.

JEWELL, P.W. (2007) – Morphology and paleoclimatic significance of Pleistocene Lake Bonneville spits. Quaternary Research, 68, 421-430.

LINDHORST, S.; BETZLER, C.; HASS, H.C. (2008) – The sedimentary architecture of a Holocene barrier spit (Sylt, Germany Bight): Swash-bar accretion and storm erosion. Sedimentary Geology, 206, 1-16.

LUIS, J.F. (2007) – Mirone: A multi-purpose tool for exploring grid data. Computers & Geosciences, 33, pp. 31-41.

LUIS, J.F. (2010) – GMT grid with the topo and bathymetry of the Algarve at ~50 m.

MOURA, D.; VEIGA-PIRES, C.; ALBARDEIRO, l., BOSKI, T.; RODRIGUES, A.L.; TARECO, H. (2007) – Holocene sea level fluctuations and coastal evolution in the central Algarve (southern Portugal). Marine Geology, 237, pp. 127-142.

PONZI, V.R.A. (2004) – Sedimentação Marinha. In: Neto, J.A.B., Ponzi, V.R.A. & Sichel, S.E., Introdução à Geologia Marinha. Rio de Janeiro: Editora interciência.

QUANTUM GIS DEVELOPMENT TEAM, (2011) – Quantum GIS Geographic Information System. Open Source Geospatial Foundation.

RODRIGUEZ, A.B.; ANDERSON, J.B.; BANFIELD, L.A.; TAVIANI, M.; ABDULAH, K.; and SNOW, J.N. (2000) – Identification of a -15 m Middle Wisconsin shoreline on the Texas inner continental shelf: Palaeogeography Palaeoclimatology Palaeoecology, v. 159, p. 25-43.

SIMMS, A.R.; ANDERSON, J.B.; BLUM, M. (2006) – Barrier-island aggradation via inlet migration: Mustang Island, Texas. Sedimentary geology, 187 (1-2), 105-125.

SOARES, A.M. (1993) – The ^{14}C content of marine shells: evidence for variability of the coastal upwelling of Portugal during the Holocene. In: Isotope Techniques in the Study of Past and Current Environmental Changes in the Hydrosphere and Atmosphere. Viena: International Atomic Energy Agency, p. 471-485

TANNER, W.F. (1995) – Environmental clastic granulometry. Florida Geological Survey, Special publication Nº 40.

TEIXEIRA, S.B. (1999) – Geomorfologia da zona submarina ao largo de Armação de Pêra (Algarve-Portugal). Actas da V Jornadas de Silves. Silves.

TEIXEIRA, S.B.; PINTO, C.A. (2002) – Idades radiocarbono de calcarenitos emersos e submersos na Baía de Armação de Pêra (Algarve – Portugal). Actas do XI Seminário Ibérico de Química Marinha, Universidade do Algarve, Faro.

VANNEY, J.; MOUGENOT, D. (1981) – La plateforme continentale du Portugal et les provinces adjacentes: Analyse geomorphologique. Memória dos Serviços Geológicos de Portugal, 28, 145p.

EVIDENCES AND HYPOTHESIS ABOUT THE ORIGIN AND USE OF NAUTICAL ARTIFACTS BETWEEN THE PEOPLE OF THE SAMBAQUIS (BRAZIL)

Flávio Rizzi CALIPPO
Professor at Universidade Federal do Piauí – UFPI
calippo@ufpi.edu.br

Abstract: *Archaeological evidences found along the Brazilian coast attest that this area was occupied since at least 8000 years BP by fishermen and gatherer groups who exploited the coastal aquatic environments. The shell mounds left by these groups are known as* middens. *Although it is believed that they were skilled navigators, evidences about this fact are still rare. From an approach focused on Maritime Archaeology, this study presents and discusses some evidences and hypotheses that seek to support the view that, in addition to the strong relationship with the aquatic environment, the people of* middens *appropriated or developed navigation techniques and nautical artifacts.*

Keywords: *Maritime Archaeology; Cluster Shelly; Prehistoric Navigation*

Résumé: *Le long de la côte brésilienne, des preuves archéologiques retrouvées attestent que cette région a été occupée depuis au moins 8000 ans BP, par les groupes de pêcheurs cueilleurs. Les amas coquilliers laissés par ces groupes sont connus comme les* sambaquis. *On estime que ces groupes étaient navigateurs, malgré les preuves à ce sujet sont encore rares. Dès une approche centrée sur l'archéologie maritime, sont présentés et discutés les évidences et les hypothèses qui suggèrent une relation forte avec le milieu aquatique et que les peuples des* sambaquis *ont utilisé des techniques de navigation et des artefacts nautiques.*

Mots-clés: *Archéologie Maritime; Amas Coquillier; Navigation Préhistorique*

INTRODUCTION

For nearly 8000 years the people of the shell mounds were distributed over a wide coastal area, dominating much of the coastal regions and water bodies that currently make up the Brazilian coast. In this process, the people of the shell middens (or the people of sambaquis) may have developed or appropriated nautical technologies. Although the employment of vessels is almost a consensus among Brazilian researchers, there are rare references on this subject in the archaeological literature. In this paper, we point out some evidences and hypotheses about the origin and use of these practices among sambaquis, and hence the ways by which they would culturally appropriate the sea and the aquatic environments.

Overall, this evidences relate to two sets of data, which relate primarily to bioarchaeological aspects and the occurrence of nautical artifacts in regions of South America, in prior or contemporary periods assigned to age of the middens. A dataset that even indirectly can attest to the development and adoption of technologies and nautical knowledge related to the arts of navigation.

In this article, such evidence is interpreted from a Maritime Archaeology, as suggested by Adams (2002). It seeks to transcend the limits of marine environments, and analyzes the various material manifestations of their cultures from their interactions with the various types of aquatic environments.

Although understanding Adams *(op. cit.)* constitutes a proposition as yet unspoilt by itself maritime archeology, it is adopted and developed here because it taises new possibilities to create an interpretation about a way of life whose social, cultural or symbolic practices can be associated to both sea and land.

From the theoretical point of view, such proposal can be seen as a continuation of maritime archeology created by Keith Muckelroy that, in late 1970, seeking to overcome the historical-culturalist then prevalent in archeology practice at sea, proposed that archaeologists begin to establish as their main objective of study the man and no more artifacts (ships, cargoes, etc...) lost at sea. Muckelroy (1978) emphasized that, in this process, it should be also taken into consideration everything that was connected with life at sea and not only the remains of ships and boats found therein.

Based on maritime archeology developed by Muckelroy, Adams (2002) suggests a more comprehensive approach, which, while it surpasses the understanding of fisheries and toil of the sea as a distinct sub-culture, it allows both maritime and land evidence to be used to understand the maritime universe and the relations the people established with the sea (Calippo, 2011).

In this sense, Adams' proposal aligns with a new chain of Maritime Archaeology, according to Duran (2008, p. 92), that seeks to break with the geographical limitations of the underwater world, with specific focus on the sites of shipwrecks and the inclusion of earthly elements associated, in one way or another, to the sea universe. The sites covered by maritime archeology would be found both on land and at sea, and more than the environment in which they occur (or the way we use to access them), what matters most is the understanding of the processes and correlations with the marine universe that are preserved inside (Fontenoy, 1998).

From this point of view, the consequences of a maritime culture would not end exactly on the last remnant salt water bathing beach or shoreline from different islands and continents. It would extend their influence inland, also encompassing equipment, production and religious structures, and even entire cities (Duran, op. cit., p. 92).

> [...] those 'related objects on the shore' and 'coastal communities' explicitly ruled out by Keith Muckelroy would just as explicitly be ruled in today. Indeed, it is through them that coastal and sea-born maritime concerns articulate with society at large. Today, then, maritime archaeology is the study of material (Adams, 2002, p. 328).

Thus, they should compose the sea universe of shellmounds people not only the ocean and marine environments, but also all those aquatic environments associated with the coastal region, being concerned as intrinsic to the universe all marine environments perceived and culturally appropriate for shellmounds people, regardless of how close they were to the sea (Calippo, 2011).

Although it is believed here that the sambaquis people could construct their own views about these different "wet" compartments and also about the various emerged regions, it is important to note that the current subdivision of these areas (in marine, ocean, lakes, estuaries, etc.) and the "prejudices" of interpretation which are created in relation to them, are, in a sense, influenced by the way we, archaeologists understand the aquatic environments.

According to "Blot (1999), Read (1996) and Rambelli (2003), in most cases, these understandings should be a reflection of the influence of how our society culturally conceives the sea. This design is not restricted only to Brazilian issues, because the separation between maritime and continental perpetuated due to the fact that "in western societies, the sea remains is understood as a space known evil, dangerous, out of crop land, outside the law prevailing on the continent" (Diegues, 1998, p. 58). In this process, one can identify a kind of "resistance" when we look at the sea, because "underwater region becomes thus a symbol of the unconscious" (Diegues, 2000, p. 159; Rambelli, 2003, p. 12).

As in this article we seek to identify and discuss various types of archaeological data as evidences of the use of nautical artifacts by people of middens, we cannot, from this perspective of maritime archeology, fail to consider the correlation of vessels and navigation with social practices (economic and symbolic) developed by sambaquis. For Malinowski (1984, p. 87), for example, the boat was not just an artifact or a vehicle through which the native wander between the islands. "It is involved in an atmosphere of romance, made up of traditions and personal experiences" (Malinowski, 1984, p. 87).

According to this author, however there was a social organization underlying the construction of vessels, it was not built only by individuals (leading specialists and workers) whose task was to build canoes, browse them and support the *kula*. The specialist (which can be more than one), the same way that has the knowledge to build a canoe and make the slots, is also responsible for performing magic. For the Trobriand islanders, besides the construction of canoes, is the magic that provides navigation, rescue, *kula,* trade, fishing and gathering of the most important means (Malinowski, *ibid,* p. 94). In this sense the canoe is not only an artifact used for navigation, it "Is the powerful tool which allows them to become masters of nature, able to thrive in demand dangerous seas to distant lands" (Malinowski, *ibid,* p. 88).

> It is an object of worship and admiration, a living thing that has its own personality. To the native, the canoe is a powerful tool that allows you to become master of nature, able to thrive in demand dangerous seas to distant lands. It's associated with travel [...] that he expressed in songs and stories (Malinowski, *op. cit.*, p. 87).

BIOARCHAEOLOGICAL EVIDENCES

The first of these sets regards to data derived from bioarchaeological studies which, based on analysis of bone abnormalities present in individuals from sambaquis, suggest the establishment of nautical activities related to the practice of diving vessels and the use of the paddle. Specifically in relation to anomalies, these can be of three types: Ear exostosis (bone abnormalities that form the base of the external auditory canal), changes in the structures of insertion of muscle bundles and bone irregular wear.

According to Okumura *et al.* (2006) and Schell-Ybert *et al.* (2003), the auricular exostoses are mainly related to constant immersion in cold water and salted wind exposure. What would indicate a certain adaptability and mastery of techniques associated with diving by the sambaquis. By analyzing the exostosis at sambaqui Jabuticabeira II (Santa Catarina), Okumura *(op. cit,* p. 275) indicates that such anomalies would be more common in males.

> This type of exostoses is reported to be caused by frequent dives in cool (Chaplin e Stewart, 1998; Kennedy, 1986) or salt water (Peixoto, 1989).

Regarding the modification of the structures of insertion of muscle bundles and irregular wear bone, Carvalho

(2004) suggests an association of these anomalies to practical activities related to swimming, the use of paddles (standing and sitting) and, indirectly, the manufacture of canoes.

Based on the analysis of the joints of shell middens of Santa Catarina and Rio de Janeiro, Carvalho (2004, p. 152) points out that the most affected joint sets are, respectively, wrist and elbow. Among the prehistoric populations, according to the author, "the great involvement of the wrist should be linked primarily to movements involving the same time, firmness, and mobility in the region, [...], as occurs, for example in manufactured goods (polishing, scraping), in activities involving reduction of raw material or [in preparation] food (scraping, grinding)" (Carvalho, *op. cit,* p. 152). Activities also held throughout the manufacturing process of canoes and boats.

In the case of the elbow joint stress, it is likely that would be associated with "[...] the carriage weight or flexion / extension of the forearm against any resistance, as may occur in stroke and drag chains, for example" (Carvalho, *ibid*, p. 152).

Next to the wrist and elbow, according to the author, the link that has the highest wear is the shoulder. While in the background, means, based on the result of this analysis, that such joint changes also indicate some relationship to the practice of nautical activities (throwing harpoons and spears), the manufacture of canoes (axes and adzes) and those related to aquatic environments (swimming), because:

> The shoulder is particularly sensitive to activities that involve movements of large extension above the head as throwing objects, modern swimming and application of different strokes accompanied by various tools (such as axes, hammers, clubs, etc..) and associated with large movements (Carvalho, 2004, p. 155 *apud* Whiting and Zernicke, 2001).

The ankle "was one of the least affected joints in the series studied and, as has [...] an indispensable role in the march and support the body weight" (Carvalho, 2004, p. 156), the author suggests that there may have been less effort due to activities such as walking on the use of boats.

Regarding to muscular stress markers, Carvalho aims to maintain the same standard which, in general, is related to greater use of the upper limbs compared to the lower ones. In the upper *limbs,* "[...] movements involving the whole arm / shoulder must have been frequent in all series, emphasized the development of the insertion of the deltoid and pectoralis major" (Carvalho, *op. cit,* p. 162). According to the author, the development of corresponding areas of muscle attachment is associated with various activities such as "[...] the use of double oars, the removal of animal skins, handling tools such as axes [to manufacture canoes], hoes, pickaxes, the use of large pylons in swimming (especially in modern swimming movements), the throwing of objects, among others" (Carvalho, *ibid*, p. 156).

Another request was fairly muscle biceps, which is also related to the use of oars. Capasso (1999) and Hawkey and Merbs (1995) indicate that the development "[...] that bilateral muscle is often related to the loading of weights with the arm flexed and the use of oars double" (Carvalho, 2004, p. 162). Activity – rowing – is also indicated as a result of the indexes obtained in strength of the people from sambaquis over the pronator quadratus muscle. The author relates also to use these muscles in activities related to "[...] food processing by grinding or scraping, polishing the different artifacts [as the blades of the ax] and other movements that can be performed with the elbow flexed and the forearm in pronation" (Carvalho, *op. cit.*, p. 162).

In the case of the triceps, "[...] once again handling oars may be an explanation, along with the use of [...] axes, [...] long spears or harpoons, accompanied by a pitch fast and within walking distance of the target, which could be associated with fishing in calm waters and good visibility" (Carvalho, *ibid*, p. 163). The author draws attention also to:

> [...] the use of vessels that requires long rods as propellants [for rafts and canoes] and oars, common kind of transport in calm waters with little current, where the driver usually stands upright and the effort is shared between both arms. Should not be disregarded, however, the use of axes (Carvalho, *ibidem*, p. 163).

In the conclusion of his analysis, the author also indicates that the effort devoted to the use of harpoons, thrusters, bows, spears and so on, did not surpass the effort devoted to activities such as the use of boats and fishing nets" (Carvalho, *ibid*, p. 170). Suggesting that although all sambaquis communities have maintained contact with aquatic environments, this relationship has not only given from their shores. It is likely that, effectively, the sambaquis have broken the land-sea boundary, venturing amid lagoons and coastal waters.

THE EARLIEST EVIDENCE OF NAVIGATION IN SOUTH AMERICA

Although Carvalho (2004) has suggested the use of different types of boats (canoes and rafts) and thrusters (oars, paddles double sticks and rods), other types of nautical artifacts, some technologically simpler, which may indicate not only the adoption of a nautical technology, but also its development by people sambaquis.

Such a perspective is difficult to be considered when dealing with more complex vessels, which are formed from the linkage of several technological innovations that transform them into artefacts, whose construction and use require the work of specialists. However, when we refer

Figure 1 – Representation of a Kaveri River *fisherman (South India) using a float swimming*

to parts nautical simplest perhaps the development possibility of navigation can be compared to the development of any type of prehistoric technology.

When we think of a Brazilian prehistoric vessel the most common image is that of a canoe. However, there are many other floats artifacts that could be employed in fishing and in everyday sambaquis they did not require necessarily the same degree of technological expertise employed in canoes. Some even neither could be considered vessels.

Although there is no precise division between them, Hornell (1970) suggests a subdivision of the floats into two categories: swimming floats *(swimming floats)* and propelled floats *(riding floats)*.

The swimming floats accessories are simpler, like small pieces of wood, logs, bags of skin, etc., used to assist the fluctuation of the body while the individual remains stationary, or follow the whim of the current or moves with a propulsion and direction generated by their feathers and arms (figure 1). A tree following downstream, according to Hornell *(op. cit,* p. 1.), was the first stimulus to the inventiveness of man in this direction.

In propelled floats, on the other hand, instead of one individual (and only one) being immersed, a group remained on a log or beam and reed, and, besides the members of the group, they also used propellants sticks, rods, paddles, etc...

There are several examples of the use of floats by fisher populations by traditional Indian natives and throughout the world. In Australia, for example, according to Stokes (1846, p. 11, 15-16), there are numerous examples of Aboriginal use of logs as swimming floats. They are often found along the north coast of Australia, where the aborigines use a small log or piece of wood strapped to his chest, to make long journeys between the islands and the mainland. In America, Mason (1895, p. 334) indicates the use of a float of wood as a practice of tribes of the Gulf of California to rest your arms when they swim.

Hornell (op. cit.) States that a minimum definition of floats cannot be presented without a reference on the Hawaiian surfboards. Although they are now used for sports practice, Lisiansky (1814), who visited the island in 1804, saw no canoes there, but many natives came to the boat using each, a wooden plank.

From the technological point of view, it would be impossible for sambaquis to have developed and used floats and, from this nautical trial (mainly done in the first moments of the Sambaquieira occupation, where they would be adapting to coastal environments), developed innovations that led to building rafts and floats for processing in canoes. In addition to having sufficient knowledge to their construction, the patterns of joint and muscle stress, indicated by Carvalho (2004), as described in the previous section, are also consistent with the use of both types of floats and propulsion elements of construction of canoes.

Although there is still a lot of material evidence with which to discuss the development of Sambaquieira nautical technology, depending on these arguments, we cannot deny it. Accordingly, we hold that both the navigation and the construction of floats, rafts and canoes could have been developed by people from middens, as well as have been developed by other people along the current Brazilian territory, South America and around the world.

Once established, among sambaquis, the technologies needed for the preparation of the floats, the next step in the technological development of the vessels should be associated with the transformation in these rafts and dugouts (pirogues, monoxylon or logboat). Hornell (1970, p. 1) that points, to the emergence of barges or rafts, it would be enough that the logs or bundles of reeds were tied together, side by side.

Regarding the more complex nautical artifacts, developed from techniques that supersede the excavation, modeling and aggregation of floats (as occurs, for example, in the construction of boats, where different types of structures are joined to form a hull), it is more likely that such technological development has not been reached by sambaquis. Besides not being met a tooling that would allow the construction of these types of vessels, such boats are not found even among the societies that subsequently came to inhabit the areas previously occupied by sambaquis.

Returning to the question of simpler nautical artifacts, Carabias (2000) highlights a number of pre-Hispanic evidence of navigation along the northern coast of Chile. The oldest material trace browsing this relates to a miniature raft totora (reed) found in a "[...] *cementerio de túmulos, ubicado 6 km al sur de La desembocadura del rio Loa, fechada em 215 d.C."* (figure 2) (Carabias, 2000, p. 34 *apud* Llagostera, 1990).

However, the countryside of Brazil is where may be the oldest evidence of manufacture and construction of

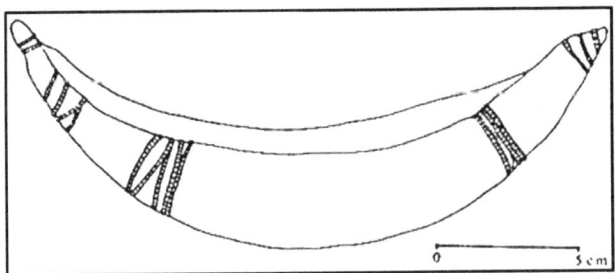

Figure 2 – Thumbnail of the raft of reeds found in northern Chile (Carabias, op. cit., p. 34)

Figure 3 – Casa Santa archaeological site, in Carnaúba dos Dantas, Rio Grande do Norte, Brazil (Borges, 2008)

canoes, which helps to refute the understandings that the nautical technology could only have come to South America after being developed by people and technology culturally more advanced. In fact, even if the navigation has not arisen independently, the more likely it is that in every community or village where new groups began to use such technology, she was constantly modified based innovations and insights developed based on trial of individuals and groups to which they belonged.

> *En um comienzo, el tema de ela navegación en América sirvió para alimentar inconsistentes hipótesis difusionistas de poblamiento; largos viajes "oceánicos" fueran señalados como un mecanismo mediante el cual agentes "civilazadores" venidos desde tierras distantes, com un mayor nivel de desarrollo sociocultural, hicieron entrega de aparataje tecnológico y empleo de técnicas a otros grupos com niveles supuestamente más "atrasados"* (Carabias, 2000, p. 31)

This evidence relates to a series of representations of canoes (figures 3-7) classified as tradition northeast, which were painted in rock shelters of Seridó region, in the state of Rio Grande do Norte. A tradition that, according to Borges (2008, p. 12), would have remained in the region between 12,000 and 6,000 years BP.

Although Martin (1997) refers to canoes, an analysis directed to the nautical theme not only suggests the possibility of such paintings represent dugout canoes, but mainly due to its semi-lunar shape, indicate canoes sheaves of reeds or tree bark. These representations are still possible to identify a recurrence of accessory elements, which could be related to adaptations or innovations resulting from experimentation and continuous development of these vessels.

In addition to possible use of a mast and is not necessarily linked to survival (figure 8 – c) representations suggest the possibility of using any type of canopy (figure 08 – g). Even though this kind of form of geometric representation is common in sites of the region and, in this sense, a misinterpretation can be established from the superposition of different figures, its association with one of the masts further strengthens the hypothesis of this element represent a canoe with some kind of sail propulsion.

Figure 4 – Probable representation of a pirogue (classified as the Nordeste Tradition) in a rock shelter in Seridó region, in Rio Grande do Norte, Brazil (photo: Flávio Calippo)

Figure 5 – Probable representation of a pirogue (classified as the Nordeste Tradition) in a rock shelter in Seridó region, in Rio Grande do Norte, Brazil (photo: Flávio Calippo)

Figure 6 – Probable representation of a pirogue (classified as the Nordeste *Tradition) in a rock shelter in* Seridó *region, in* Rio Grande do Norte, *Brazil (photo: Flávio Calippo)*

Figure 7 – Probable representation of a pirogue (classified as the Nordeste *Tradition) in a rock shelter in* Seridó *region, in* Rio Grande do Norte, *Brazil (photo: Flávio Calippo)*

Figure 8 – Representation of dogout canoes found in the Pedra do Alexandre *archaeological site, in* Carnauba dos Dantas, Rio Grande do Norte, *Brazil (c – representation of a canoe that carries seven people led by a chief who sports long feather headdress; g: probable representation of a sail) (Martin, 1997, p. 255)*

While here we defend the possibility of such representations be related to canoes with certain types of innovations (masts, sails, etc.) or adaptations developed to local needs, years later, according to Borges (2008, p. 52), Gabriela Martin and Anne Marie Pessis pointed out, based on comparative ethnographic analysis, the possibility of these images are also representations of networks funeral.

Despite the attribution of meaning to this type of graphic be a rather controversial issue, it would at least require a special study of this question, there are some characteristics that allow us to hypothesize about the use of vessels associated with the archaeological context of Seridó region. In addition sails representations of likely meet recurrently associated with canoes and possible masts, these candles have a pattern apparently different from those found in other geometrical figures (fringes), which are distributed by the panels in the region sites (figure 3). Moreover, even if such figures could not be so considered, and the nautical theme as a reference, perhaps, may represent the use of fishing nets.

Even if still it is not possible to have a more specific and precise sense for this issue, there is another factor that fosters the understanding of these representations as canoes: the paleoenvironmental context of Seridó region. According to Borges *(op. cit,* p. 66), the region is marked by a sharp relief, by which develops a drainage intermittent, in which the region's rivers only assume their maximum volumes along the rainy seasons. However, according to this author, several archaeological evidence (records rock and trace food) suggests the predominance, in the past, an environment punctuated by a water regime more prominent than the current one.

When addressing the issue of the origin of the occupation of the hinterland Seridó, in both cases it proposes (via rivers or inland from the coast), the aquatic environment is always the main connecting factor.

A similar situation was presented by Carabias (2000, p. 40), when addressing the question of the origin of the ferries used for ocean navigation prehistoric along the Pacific coast:

Evidencias arqueológicas apuntam a contactos marítimos periódicos entre el litoral ecuatoriano y Mesoamérica desde el Período Formativo Temprano, em tempos tan antiguos como La fase Valdivia Tardia (ca. 2.000-1.500 a.C.), pero se cree que los précerámisco Valdivia que arribaron al lugar, yaposeían embarcaciones de alta mar (ca. 3.400 a.C.) (Zeidler, 1986). Buse (1973), há postulado que las balsas de madera se genaron em los rios interiores Del Perú, sufriendo uma posterior adaptacion marítima (Carabias, ibidem, p. 40).*

CONCLUSION

Based on the assumptions and the data discussed here about the relationship of the first inhabitants of the Brazilian coast with the aquatic environments, we cannot fail to consider the existence of archaeological evidence in this regard. Although some of this evidence and hypotheses still have points that should be further explored, we know that there is a theoretical approach that is able to identify and understand such evidence. This article represents a first look at targeting these issues.

To continue to this discussion we need to go forward looking at the shellmounds people also seeking to understand them from a dialectical relationship with the aquatic environments where individuals, to interact with this medium, both altered coastal environments and passed through experiences that changed them individually and collectively. A process that probably left traces and may indicate the perceptions and strategies that sambaquis developed to dominate the coastal and aquatic environments.

References

ADAMS, Jonathan (2002) – Maritime Archaeology. In: Charles E. Orser, Jr (Ed.). Encyclopedia of Historical Archaeology. London: Routledge, 2002, p. 328-330.

BLOT, Jean-Yves (1999) – O mar de Keith Muckelroy: o papel da teoria na arqueologia do mundo náutico. Al-Madan, Almada, Centro de Arqueologia, série 2, n. 8, p. 41-55, out. 1999.

BORGES, Cláudia Cristina do Lago (2008) – Uma narrativa pré-histórica. O cotidiano de antigos grupos humanos no sertão do Seridó/RN. Tese de Doutorado em História. Universidade Estadual Paulista. Assis. 182 p.

CALIPPO, Flávio Rizzi (2011) – Sociedade Sambaquieira, Comunidades Marítimas. Revista de Arqueologia (Sociedade de Arqueologia Brasileira), v.34, p. 1-20.

CAPASSO, L.; KENNEDY, K.A.R.; WILCZAK, C.A. (1999) – Atlas of Occupational Markers on Human Remains. Teramo: Edigrafital S.P.A.

CARABIAS, Diego (2000) – Navegación prehispánica em el Norte de Chile: uma contribución al estúdio de lãs práticas náuicas em lãs áreas Andes Centro-Sur y Meridional. Revista Werkén, n° 1, octobre. Santiago, p. 31-53.

CARVALHO, Claudia Rodrigues (2004) – Marcadores de estresse ocupacional em populações sambaquieiras no litoral fluminense. 2004. Tese (Doutorado em Saúde Pública) – Escola Nacional de Saúde Pública, Rio de Janeiro.

CHAPLIN J.M.; STEWART, I.A. (1998) – The prevalence of exostoses in the external auditory meatus of surfers. Clin Otolaryngol, 23-24, p. 326-330.

DIEGUES, Antônio Carlos Sant'Ana (1998) – Ilhas e mares: simbolismo e imaginário. São Paulo: Editora Hucitec.

DIEGUES, Antonio Carlos Sant'Ana (2000) – Os ex-votos marítimos da sala de milagres da Basílica do Senhor Bom Jesus de Iguape, São Paulo. In: Antonio Carlos Sant'AnaDiegues (Org.). A imagem das águas. São Paulo: Hucitec, p. 157-207.

DURAN, Leandro D. (2008) – Arqueologia Marítima de Um Bom Abrigo. Tese (Doutorado em Arqueologia) – Museu de Etnologia e Arqueologia, Universidade de São Paulo, São Paulo, 2008, p. 338.

FONTENOY, Paul (1998) – A Discussion of Maritime Archaeology. In: Babits, Lawrence; Tilburg, Hans Van (Eds.). Maritime Archaeology – A Reader of Substantive and Theoretical Contributions. New York: Plenum Press (The Plenum Series in Underwater Archaeology).

HAWKEY, D.E. & MERBS, C.F. (1995) – Activity-induced musculoskeletal stress markers (MSM) and subsistence strategy among ancient Hudson Bay Eskimos. International Journal of Osteoarchaeology, 5: 324-338.

HORNELL, James (1970) – Water Transportation: origins & early evolution. David & Charles: Newton Abbot.

KENNEDY, G.E. (1986) – The relationship between exostoses and cold water: a latitudinal analysis. Am J. Phys Anthrop, 71-74, p. 401-415. Lisiansky, U. (1806) – A Voyage round the World. 1803-1806.

LLAGOSTERA, A. (1990) – La navegación prehispánica en el Norte de Chile: bioindicadores e inferencias teóricas. Chungará, 24-25, p. 37-51. Malinowski, Bronislaw (1984) – Argonautas do Pacífico Ocidental. Um relato do empreendimento e da aventura dos nativos nos arquipélagos da Nova Guiné Melanésia. Ed. Abril Cultural. São Paulo. 428 p.

MARTIN, Gabriela (2005) – Pré-História do Nordeste do Brasil. 4ª. ed. Recife: Universitária da UFPE, v. 1. 395 p.

MUCKELROY, Keith (1978) – Maritime Archaeology. Cambridge: Cambridge University Press, (New Studies in Archaeology).

MURDOCK, G.P. (1968) – The current status of the wourld's hunting and gathering people. In: Lee,

Richard & Devore, Irven (Eds.). Man the hunter. Chicago: Aldine. p. 13-22,

OKUMURA, M.M.M. (2005/2006) – Análise de exostose do meato auditivo externo como um marcador de atividade aquática em restos esqueletais humanos da costa e do interior do Brasil. Revista do Museu de Arqueologia, n° 15/16. Universidade de São Paulo. São Paulo, p. 181-189.

PEIXOTO, M.V. (1989) – Avaliação radiológica do *torus auditivus* nos grupos formadores de Sambaquis do litoral meridional brasileiro: contribuição ao estudo dos traços não métricos em populações pré-históricas do Brasil. MSc thesis. Depto. de Anatomia Humana. Universidade Federal do Rio de Janeiro.

RAMBELLI, Gilson (2003) – Arqueologia subaquática do Baixo Vale do Ribeira, SP, 259 p. Tese (Doutorado em arqueologia) – Museu de Arqueologia e Etnologia, Faculdade de Filosofia, Letras e Ciências Humanas – Universidade de São Paulo. São Paulo.

READ, J. (1996) – The Indian Ocean in Antiquity, London: New York, 1996.

SCHELL-YBERT, R.; EGGERS, S.; WESOLOWSKI, V.; PETRONILHO, C.C.; BOYADJIAN, C.H.; DE BLASIS, P.A.D.; BARBOSA-GUIMARÃES, M.; GASPAR, M.D. (2003) – Novas perspectives na reconstituição do modo de vida dos sambaquieiros: uma abordagem multidisciplinar. Revista de Arqueologia. Sociedade de Arqueologia Brasileira, São Paulo, v. 16, p. 109-137.

WHITING, W.C. & ZERNICKE, R.F. (2001) – Biomecânica da Lesão Musculoesquelética. Rio de Janeiro: Guanabara Koogan.

COASTLINE AND LITHIC TECHNOLOGY DURING THE TARDIGLACIAL IN THE ALGARVE

Carolina MENDONÇA & Leandro INFANTINI

Phd students, Universidade do Algarve, Núcleo de Arqueologia e Paleoecologia
mendoncarolina@gmail.com   leandroinfantini@hotmail.com

Abstract: *During the Tardiglacial, vast portions of the continental shelf of the Algarve were emerged due to variations in the sea level. In this sense, the relationship between human occupations and the territory should be interpreted taking into account the occurrence of this phenomenon. In order to better understand the size and spatial distribution of archaeological sites and interactions with the coastline, it becomes necessary to create a Geographic Information System (GIS) in order to create a picture of the paleoenvironment of this region. This study aims to examine, in a preliminary way, through the lithic technology and GIS, the relationships between changes of the shoreline of the current territory of the Algarve and the human communities that occupied the same territory, during the Tardiglacial in the Algarve.*

Keywords: *Coastline; Lithic technology; Tardiglacial; GIS*

Résumé: *Au cours du Tardiglaciaire des vastes portions du plateau continental de l'Algarve ont été émergé en raison des variations dans le niveau de la mer. Dans ce sens, la relation entre les occupations humaines et le territoire doivent être interprétés en tenant compte l'occurrence de ce phénomène. Afin de mieux comprendre la taille et la répartition spatiale des sites archéologiques et les interactions avec la ligne de côte, il devient nécessaire de créer un Système d'Information Géographique (SIG) afin de créer une image du paléoenvironnement de cette région. Cette étude vise à examiner, de façon préliminaire, les relations entre les changements de la ligne de côte de l'actuel territoire de l'Algarve et les communautés humaines qui occupaient le même territoire, par la technologie lithique au cours du Tardiglaciaire dans l'Algarve.*

Mots-clés: *Ligne de côte, technologie lithique; Tardiglaciaire; SIG*

1. INTRODUCTION

Geo-Information is a concept that covers the acquisition, processing, interpretation (or analysis) of data or information spatially referenced, such as Geographic Information System (GIS). It can be a tool for integration and analysis of archaeological data with the local or regional context aimed at explaining in which way and by whom that place or region was occupied in the past. Thus the GIS applications have a great importance for Archaeology since they allow a greater understanding of the past.

Furthermore, GIS are very important for the Geosciences, mainly for the paleoenvironment reconstruction, since it allow the design of a more precise picture of the past by using geospatial information and tools that can simulate with higher precision these paleoenvironments. In this sense, the simulation of paleocoastlines assumes great importance for the understanding of the processes related to the variation of the sea level.

This study aims an interdisciplinary approach, seeking to integrate both the usage of a geographic information system and a study of the evolution of the shoreline with some archeological sites data for the Tardiglacial in the Algarve, through the paleotechnological analysis of its lithic collections.

The region of Algarve, located in Southern Portugal, has enormous potential for the study of Prehistory and Protohistory by their geographical and climatic characteristics and in spite of the ongoing development of tourist infrastructure, demographic pressure did not have a strong impact on the transformation of the landscape (Bicho, 2006).

2. MATERIAL AND METHODS

2.1. Archaeological Sites

From the archaeological point of view, the Algarve is one of the most rich regions of Portugal, with more than 1700 archaeological sites known, although many are already destroyed or do not present enough potential for research and/or recovery. Concerning the information about the occupation of this region during the Upper Paleolithic, it essentially results from archaeological works performed in the end of the last decade of the 20th century, namely through research projects approved under the regulation of the National Plan of Archeological Works as well as "*preventive projects*" under which archaeological works took place regarding prevention and salvation of sites. These projects consisted of environmental impact assessments, urban regeneration, constraints of projects in classified museums or its protection zones, among others (Quelhas; Zambujo, 1998; Zambujo; Pires, 1999; Bicho 2003, 2004a; Bicho *et al.*, 2004a, 2004b; Manne *et al.*, 2005).

These sites are cataloged on the largest database of archaeological sites existing in Portugal, called *Endovélico*.

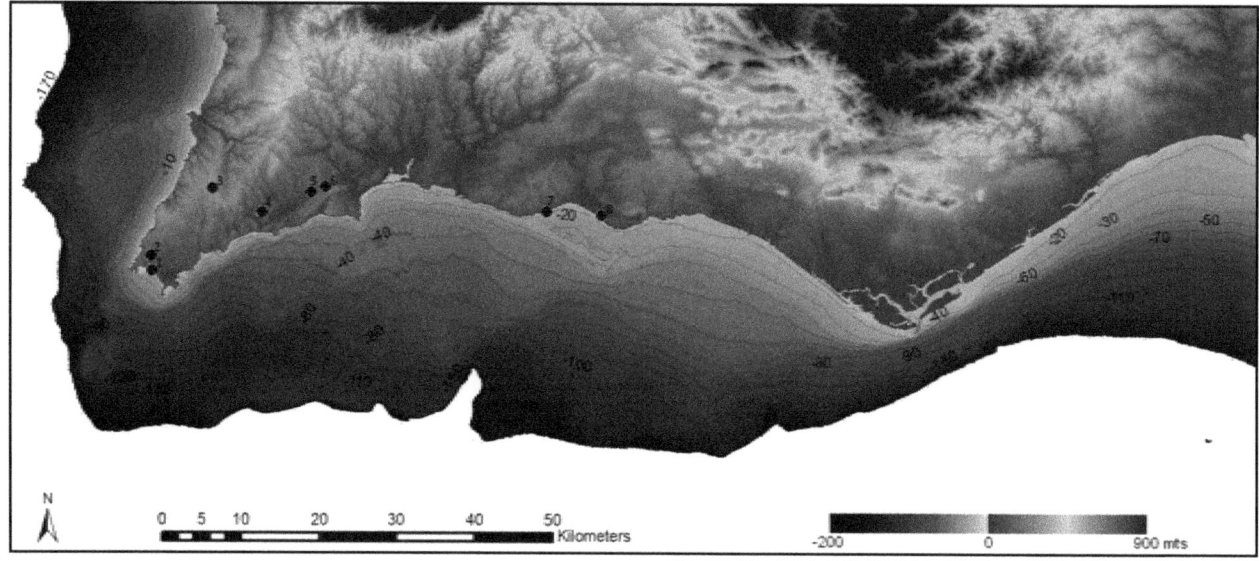

Figure 1 – Digital Terrain Model (MDT), with altimetric and bathymetric data of the Algarve, and archaeological sites in the area. 1) Ponta Garcia; 2) Vale Santo 4; 3) Lagoa do Bordoal; 4) Vale Boi; 5) Monte Januário; 6) Cruz da Pedra; 7) Praia de Albandeira; 8) Praia da Galé

This database is under the responsibility of IGESPAR (Management Institute of Architectural and Archaeological Heritage). However, the *Endovélico* manages archaeological information both of the entire country and of all periods. For better management of information on prehistoric sites of the Algarve region, it became necessary to create a spatial database. This Geographic Information System is called SIGPAL, or Geographic Information System of the Paleolithic of the Algarve (Infantini, in press).

For this research was also used digital terrain models for characterizing the altimetry and bathymetry of the region, among others. Thus, six Tardiglacial sites of the Algarve were selected for this study. They are: *Lagoa do Bordoal, Ponta Garcia, Praia de Albandeira, Praia da Galé, Vale Boi* and *Vale Santo 4,* and all located in the western area of the Algarve (Fig. 1).

2.2. Digital Terrain Model

A Digital Terrain Model (DTM) or Digital Elevation Model (DEM) can be defined as a set of numeric data support that allows to associate, in any defined point on the cartographic plan, a value corresponding to its altitude (Matos 2008). The advantage of Digital Terrain Model is the ability to produce, in addition to its altitude at any point, three-dimensional perspectives that help in simulations of the landscape.

Thereby, for the altimetry of the Algarve, was used data from the SRTM – Shuttle Radar Topography Mission – (Jarvis *et al.*, 2008). This data consisted in the application of a Radar system for obtaining a digital terrain model that covers a big part of the terrestrial globe. This DTM has a spatial resolution (a single pixel in the image) of 90 meters, that is acceptable for the analysis in question. On the other hand for the characterization of the seabed was used the bathymetry of the Algarve region (Luis, 2010), with a spatial resolution of 50 meters. Although this DTM reaches abyssal depths off the coast of the Algarve, this specific information was eliminated since the area of interest is situated above -200 meters depth.

Taking into account the data mentioned, it was possible to build a digital model of the continental shelf of the region in which can be seen the rugged submarine topography and the different slopes that result in greater or lesser variability of the shoreline according to sea level changes since the Last Glacial Maximum (LGM), resulting in large or small differences in relation to distance from the coast archaeological sites, and making it possible to simulate the (probable) paleocoastlines through the curves of sea level changes.

2.3. Sea Level Changes

During the Quaternary, climatic variations and fluctuations in sea level are one of the biggest phenomena of geological and environmental impact (Ponzi, 2004). In Portugal, about sea level changes, the work of Dias, (1987) created a variation curve of sea level since Last Glacial Maximum (LGM), covering the last eighteen millennia (Dias 2004, Dias *et al.*, 2000; Magalhães, 2001).

Despite its applicability, it is necessary to highlight the margin of error of the respective curve. However, it was considered a relative precision and accuracy in relation to sea level during the studied period making it possible to infer the relative sea level in line with the archaeological chronologies of the Tardiglacial and with the aid of a GIS to simulate the respective coastlines.

For Middle Magdalenian chronologies, between 16.000 and 14.000 BP, and the Final Magdalenian to the

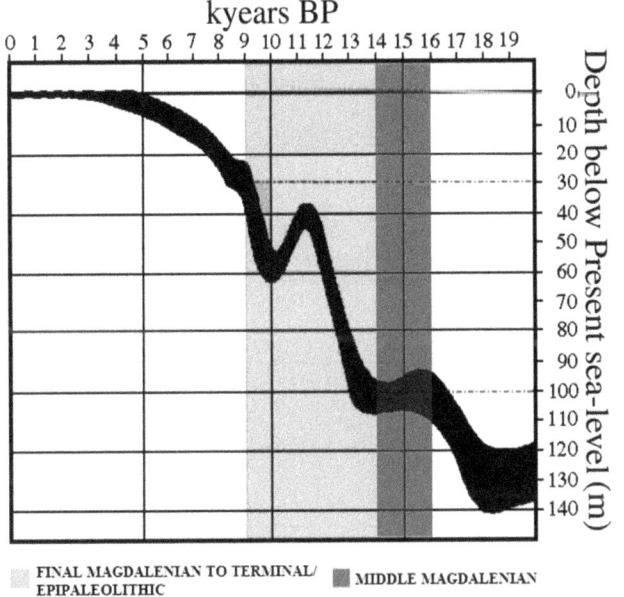

Figure 2 – Evolution of mean sea level, in the northern Portuguese continental shelf, over the past 18.000 years (Dias, 1987)

Terminal / Epipaleolithic, between 14.000 and 9.000 BP we would have different situations in relation to sea level. In the first case, the ocean level would be close to -100 meters deep, according the sea level curve (Dias et al., 2000), while in the second case there are significants paleo-environmental changes, such as the Younger Dryas, which result in large fluctuation of the ocean. In the latter case, we would have a variation of the Mean Sea Level between the current depths of -100 to -30 meters (Fig. 2).

3. ARCHAEOLOGICAL CARACTERIZATION

Given the many technological and typological analysis (performed on the selected sites), and by comparing with some of the Tardiglacial sites of Portuguese Estremadura and Spanish Magdalenian Mediterranean, also considering two other sites of the Algarve with the supposed Tardiglacial chronology – *Monte Januário* and *Cruz da Pedra* (Quelhas and Zambujo, 1998) – we would have two different chronological functions:

3.1. Middle Magdalenian – 16.000 to 14.000 BP

A more central area, dominated by a base camp (unknown) with episodic camps of the logistic type, possibly linked to the exploitation of aquatic resources (*Praia da Galé* and *Lagoa do Bordoal*), in connection with the area of Sagres for the acquisition of raw materials (Fig. 3).

3.1.1. Chaîne opératoire

Quartz and Quartzite: The preparation and maintenance occurs according to a simple and expedient reduction process, creating cores with a simple plan of percussion, bipolar and some pebble cores, with platforms predominantly cortical, from which were extracted mostly flakes. The retouched tools result in products belonging to the group of common utensils and scrapers.

Flint: The cores point to a long sequence of reduction in order to take full advantage. The cores are thoroughly explored, both for the production of flakes and for the production of bladelets.

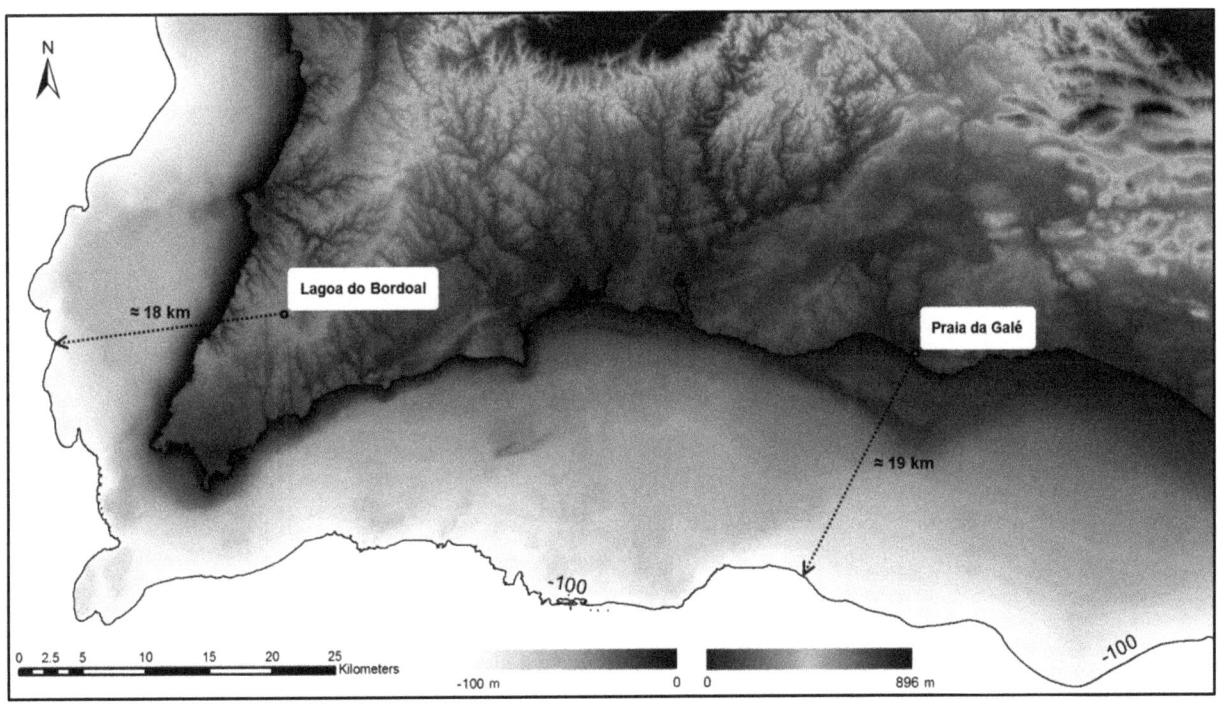

Figure 3 – Location sites of Praia da Galé and Lagoa do Bordoal and an indication of (likely) coastline to the Middle Magdalenian (-100 meters deep), demonstrating the vast territory emerged in the period

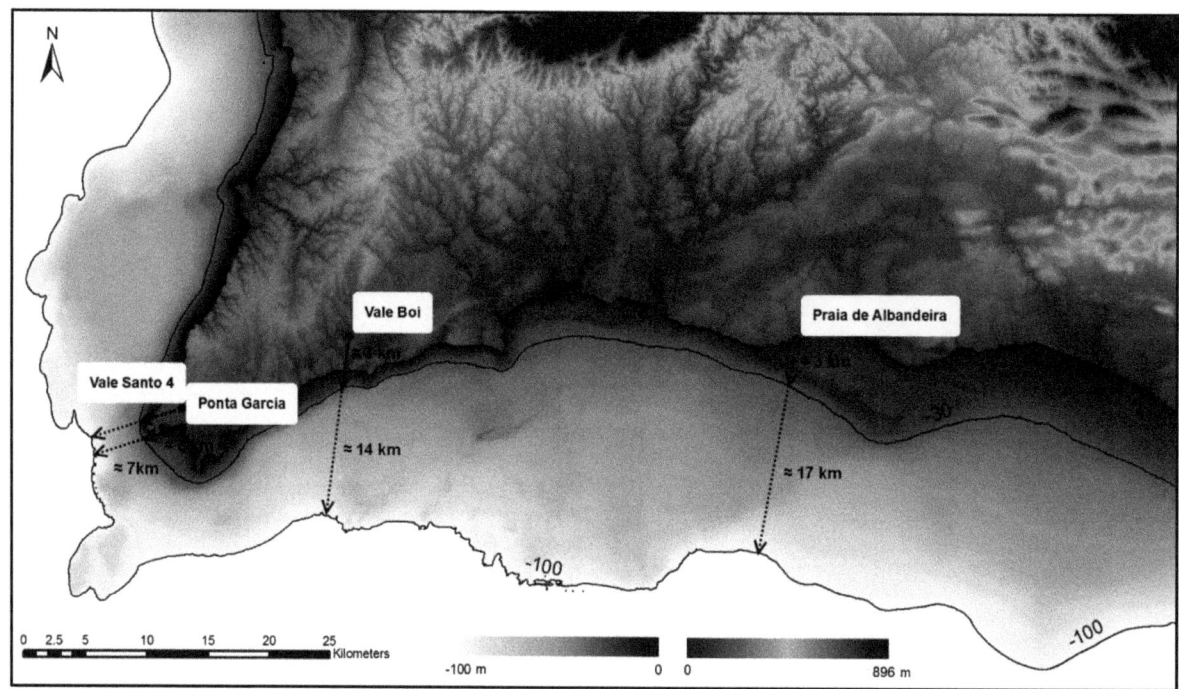

Figure 4 – Location of sites Vale Boi, Vale Santo 4, Ponta Garcia *and* Praia de Albandeira, *with their distances from the (probably) coastline between -100 m to -30 meters depth, showing the variation of the area emerged and submerged during the period*

3.2. Final Magdalenian to Terminal / Epipaleolithic – 14.000 to 9.000 BP

One area more to the southwest, dominated by the site of *Vale Boi* as base camp, with episodic camps of the logistic type related to hunting (*Cruz da Pedra* and *Monte Januário*), the acquisition of raw materials (*Vale Santo 4* and *Ponta Garcia*) and possibly linked to the exploitation of aquatic resources (*Praia de Albandeira*) (Fig. 4).

3.2.1. Chaîne Opératoire

Flint: Maintenance and preparation of cores on site. Reduction strategies resulting in simple cores with one percussion plan or orthogonal cores, with flat platform, from which were extracted mostly flakes. The retouched tools translate mainly in products belonging to the group of common utensils, scrapers, burins and backed bladelets.

Quartz, Quartzite and Greywacke: The preparation and maintenance occurs according to a simple and expedient reduction process, creating cores with a simple plan of percussion from which were extracted mostly flakes. The retouched tools essentially result in products belonging to the group of common utensils.

3.3. Functional Characterization

In the Algarve the economy of raw materials seems to be a good pointer of the chronological and spatial variability of Tardiglacial industries. The quantitative differences between sites are not only a result of lithological characteristics of the raw materials exploited, but a reflection of the type of activity practiced in each site.

The subsistence of hunter-gatherers was based on a varied range of foods where herbivorous species prevailed (Bicho, 2003; Bicho *et al.*, 2003). After a great use of malacological resources during the Gravettian at *Vale Boi*, it almost completely disappears in the Magdalenian, both in terms of food production and for personal adornment (Stiner, 2003; Bicho *et al.*, 2004B). These transformations reflect the changes occurring during this period at the geomorphological level: on the one hand, changes in sea level with the regression of the shoreline pushing the away the coastline maybe 20 kms south; on the other, the paleoenvironmental changes led to the transformation of vegetation making it more sparse in the surrounding area of *Vale Boi*.

The transformation in the habits of subsistence does not advocate the idea that aquatic resources were not used frequently, although in smaller quantities. Rather, this change in frequency of use of aquatic resources coupled with the location of sites along the coast, like the sites *Praia da Galé* and *Praia de Albandeira*, and along the season lakes such as *Lagoa do Bordoal*, seems to reflect the idea of a less residential usage of the space and more of the logistic type, thus verifying a kind of subsistence characterized by specialization.

4. FINAL DISCUSSIONS

This work has an interdisciplinary perspective, in order to try integration between studies of lithic technology with the evolution of sea level using a geographic information system. In this sense, the presented results are preliminary, as there are gaps both in identifying exactly the coastline and its respective period, as well as in dating the archaeological sites. In this sense, it is necessary to establish with more accuracy the Final Magdalenian to Terminal/Epipaleolithic sites, taking into account the high and fast changes in the sea level and environment, to identify the respective coastline and distance to the archaeological sites.

On the one hand, there is a discontinuity in the knowledge of the occupation of the territory in the Tardiglacial, since a large part of the landscape that could contain archaeological remains is presently submerged. On the other hand, it stands out in relation to the spatial distribution of the sites, and all of them being situated in the western part of the Algarve, that demonstrates the need of research and prospecting projects for the location and study of (possible) sites of the same chronology in the east as well as offshore.

Although the relative distance to the coast from the sites referenced as Middle Magdalenian, the introduction of those as logistic contexts connected to the exploration of the aquatic resources is essentially due to the paleotechnological characteristics of the lithic collections analyzed. It was also taken into consideration the establishment of the sites at the regional scale, reflecting the idea of the usage of the space more in logistic terms, characterized by specialization (Binford, 1980). Therefore, in relation to the sites considered as Lithic Workshops (*Ponta Garcia* and *Vale Santo 4*) we can still consider its short distance to the coast, therefore its usage for exploring the aquatic resources is not discarded.

In this sense, there is the possibility that major connections between the most important sites of this chronology and the exploitation of marine resources are found with the development of new research. It is believed that the results obtained in conjunction with other works of the same nature, will contribute for portraying a more reliable picture of these Paleolithic societies from the Algarve in what relates to their adaptive responses and their adapted subsistence patterns and to their interaction with the natural environment.

Acknowledgements

This work is part of the research projects of Carolina Mendonça – *A Paleotecnologia Lítica no Tardiglaciar da Península Ibérica* (SFRH/BD/65080/2009) and Leandro Infantini – *A evolução da linha de costa algarvia sob uma perspectiva arqueológica* (SFRH/BD/47538/2008), both funded by the Fundação para a Ciência e Tecnologia (FCT), Portugal.

References

AURA, J.E. (1986) – La ocupación magdaleniense de la Cueva de Nerja (la Sala de la Mina). La Prehistoria de la Cueva de Nerja (Málaga). Paleolítico y Epipaleolítico. Trabajos sobre la Cueva de Nerja. N.º 1. Málaga. p. 205-268.

AURA, J.E. (1995) – El Magdaleniense Mediterráneo: la Cova del Parpalló (Gandia, Valencia). Serie de Trabajos Varios N° 91. Valência: Servicio de Investigación Prehistórica.

AURA, J.E.; VILLAVERDE, V.; MORALES, M.G.; SAINZ, C.G.; ZILHÃO, J.; STRAUS, L.G. (1998) – The pleistocene-holocene transition in the Iberian Peninsula: continuity and change in human adaptations. Quaternary International. Volumes 49-50. p. 87-103.

BICHO, N. (1998) – Pleistocene transition in Portuguese Prehistory: a technological perspective. The Organization of Lithic Technology in Late and early Postglacial Europe. Oxford: BAR. p. 39-62.

BICHO, N. (2002a) – Lithic Raw Material Economy and Hunter-Gather Mobility in the Glacial and Early Postglacial in Portuguese Prehistory: a technological perspective. Lithic Raw Material Economies in Late Glacial and Early Postglacial Europe. Oxford: BAR. p. 161-179.

BICHO, N. (2003) – A importância dos recursos aquáticos na economia dos caçadores-recolectores do Paleolítico e Epipaleolítico do Algarve. Xelb 3 (Actas do I Encontro de Arqueologia do Algarve). Silves. p. 11-26.

BICHO, N. (2004a) – As comunidades humanas de caçadores-recolectores do Algarve Ocidental – perspective ecológica. Evolução Geohistórica do Litoral Português e Fenómenos Correlativos (Actas – Geologia, História Arqueologia e Climatologia). Lisboa: Universidade Aberta. p. 359-396.

BICHO, N. (2004b) – A Ocupação Paleolítica e Mesolítica do Algarve. Promontoria Monográfica 1. Faro: Centro de Estudos de Património – Departamento de História, Arqueologia e Património, Universidade do Algarve. p. 19-24.

BICHO, N. (2006a) – A Pré-História do Algarve. Território da Pré-História em Portugal 9. Tomar: ARKEOS.

BICHO, N. (2006b) – Manual de Arqueologia Pré-Histórica. Lisboa: Edições 70.

BICHO, N. (2009) – On the Edge: Early Holocene Adaptations in Southwestern Iberia. Journal of Anthropological Research. Volume 65. p. 185-206.

BICHO, N.; HAWS, J. (2008) – At the land's end: marine resources and the importance of fluctuations in the coast line in the prehistoric hunter-gatherer economy of Portugal. Quaternary Science Review. 27. p. 2166-2175.

BICHO, N.; STINER, M.; LINDLY, J. (2004a) – Shell Ornaments, bone tools and long distance connections in the Upper Paleolithic of Southern Portugal. La Spiritualité. Liége: ERAUL. p. 71-80.

BICHO, N.; STINER, M.; LINDLY, J. (2004b) – Notícia preliminar das ocupações humanas do sítio de Vale Boi, Vila do Bispo. Arqueologia e História, 55. p. 12-23.

BICHO, N.; CASCALHEIRA, J.; CORTÉS, M; GIBAJA, J.; ÉVORA, M.; MANNE, T.; MARREIROS, J.; MENDONÇA, C.; PEREIRA, T.; REGALA, F. (2009) – Identidade e adaptação: A ocupação humana durante o plistocénico final no Algarve. Actas da VII Reunião do Quaternário Ibérico – "O futuro do ambiente da Península Ibérica – As lições do passado geológico recente. Faro: CIMA/Universidade do Algarve. p. 171-174.

BICHO, N.; MANNE, T.; CASCALHEIRA, J.; MENDONÇA, C.; ÉVORA, M.; GIBAJA, J.; PEREIRA, T. (2010) – O Paleolítico Superior do Sudoeste da Península Ibérica: o caso do Algarve. Actas das Jornadas Internacionales sobre el Paleolítico Superior Peninsular. Novedades del S.XXI. Barcelona: Seminari d'Estudis i Recerques Prehistòriques (S.E.R.P.) Universitat de Barcelona. p. 219-238.

BINFORD, L. (1980) – Willow smoke and dog´s tails: hunter-gatherer settlement systems and archaeological site formation. American Antiquity, 31 (2). p. 2-15.

DIAS, J.A. (2004) – "A história da evolução do litoral português nos últimos vinte milénios", Evolução Geohistórica do litoral português e fenómenos correlativos: Geologia, História, Arqueologia e Climatologia, (Cardoso, L.C., Tavares, A.A.; Tavares, M.J.F., eds), Lisboa, pp. 157-170.

DIAS, J.M.A.; BOSKI, T.; RODRIGUES, A.; MAGALHÃES, F. (2000) – Coast line Evolution in Portugal since the Last Glacial Maximum until Present – A Synthesis. Marine Geology, pp. 170:177-186.

DIVISÃO DE INVENTÁRIO DO INSTITUTO PORTUGUÊS DE ARQUEOLOGIA, (2002). – Endovélico: Sistema de Gestão e Informação Arqueológica, Revista Portuguesa de Arqueologia, Vol. 5, Nº 1, (pp. 277-283). Lisboa: IPA.

FORREST, B.; RINK, W.J.; BICHO, N.; FERRING, F. (2003) – OSL Ages and possible bioturbation signals at the Upper Paleolithic site of Lagoa do Bordoal, Algarve, Portugal. Quaternary Sicence Review 22. p. 1279-1285.

JARVIS, A.; REUTER, H.I.; NELSON, A.; GUEVARA, E. (2008) – Hole-filled SRTM for the globe Version 4, available from the CGIAR-CSI SRTM 90 m.

INFANTINI, L. – (in press) – Sistema de Informação Geográfica para a Pré-história do Algarve. Actas da IV Jornadas de Jovens em Investigação Arqueológica, Faro.

LUIS, J.F. (2010) – GMT grid with the topo and bathymetry of the Algarve at ~50 m.

MAGALHÃES, Fernando M.Q. (2001) – Os Sedimentos da Plataforma Continental Portugal: Contrastes espaciais, perspectiva temporal, potencialidades económicas, Lisboa.

MANNE, T.; STINER, M.; BICHO, N. (2005) – Evidence for Resource Intensification in Algarve (Portugal) During the Upper Paleolithic. Animais na Pré-História e Arqueologia da Península Ibérica (Actas do IV Congresso de Arqueologia Peninsular). Faro: Centro de Estudos de Património – Departamento de História, Arqueologia e Património, Universidade do Algarve. pp. 145-158.

MENDONÇA, C. (2008) – O Magdalenense no Algarve: Ponta Garcia (Vila do Bispo). XELB 8 (Actas do 5º encontro de arqueologia do Algarve). Câmara Municipal de Silves: Silves. p. 9-26.

MENDONÇA, C. (2009a) – A Tecnologia Lítica no Tardiglaciar do Algarve: Resultados preliminares. Actas de las Jornadas de Investigación arqueológica – Dialogando com la cultura. Tomo I. Universidad Complutense de Madrid. pp. 65-70.

MENDONÇA, C. (2009b) – A Tecnologia lítica no Tardiglaciar do Algarve. Tese de Mestrado em Arqueologia, Teoria e Métodos pela Universidade do Algarve, Faro.

MENDONÇA, C. (2010) – A Tecnologia Lítica no Tardiglaciar do Algarve: o sítio da Praia de Albandeira (Lagoa). XELB 10 (Actas do 7º encontro de arqueologia do Algarve). Câmara Municipal de Silves: Silves. p. 681-693.

PONZI, V.R.A. (2004) – "Sedimentação Marinha", Introdução à Geologia Marinha (Neto, J.; Ponzi, V.; Sichel, S., eds), Rio de Janeiro, pp. 219-242.

QUELHAS, A.; ZAMBUJO, G. (1998) – Jazidas paleolíticas no concelho de Lagos (Algarve): abordagem preliminar. Revista Portuguesa de Arqueologia. Volume 1. Número 2. Lisboa: IPA. pp. 5-18.

STINER, M. (2003) – Zooarchaeological evidence for resource intensification in Algarve, Southern Portugal. Promontoria 1. Faro: Centro de Estudos de Património – Departamento de História, Arqueologia e Património, Universidade do Algarve. pp. 27-61.

VERÍSSIMO, H. (2004) – Jazidas siliciosas da região de Vila do Bispo (Algarve). Promontoria 2. Faro: Centro de Estudos de Património – Departamento de História, Arqueologia e Património, Universidade do Algarve. p. 35-48.

VERÍSSIMO, H. (2005) – Aprovisionamento de matérias-primas líticas na Pré-história do Concelho de Vila do Bispo. O Paleolítico (Actas do IV Congresso de Arqueologia Peninsular). Faro: Centro de Estudos de Património – Departamento de História, Arqueologia e Património, Universidade do Algarve. pp. 509-523.

ZAMBUJO, G.; PIRES, A. (1999) – O sítio arqueológico da Vala, Silves: Paleolítico Superior e Neolítico Antigo. Revista Portuguesa de Arqueologia. Volume 2. Número 1. Lisboa: IPA. p. 5-24.

LEGISLATION, METHODOLOGIES AND APPLIED SCIENCES

THE IMPORTANCE OF GIS IN UNDERWATER ARCHAEOLOGY

Alexandra FIGUEIREDO
Instituto Politécnico de Tomar
alexfiga@ipt.pt

Isabel BERNARDES
Verein für Unterwasserarchäologie Berlin-Brandenburg
isabelbernardes90@gmail.com

Abstract: *GIS has developed to become a useful tool in the recording and management of data from archaeological projects. It is important for archaeology to have at its disposal an instrument that, in a very simple way, permits the display of information about the location, orientation, and position of artifacts in archaeological sites and the relation of these sites to each other.*

This work describes the importance of this tool in the relatively young science that is underwater archaeology, especially given that the use of GIS has extended to the various sub-disciplines within archaeology as a whole.

Key-words: *GIS, Underwater Archaeology, Methodology*

Résumé: *SIG développé pour un outil utile pour enregistrer et gérer des données provenant de projets archéologiques. Il est important pour l'archéologie de posséder un instrument qui permet l'affichage de information surf emplacement, orientation et des artifacts position du context des sites archéologiques en rapport à l'autre, d'une manière tout simplement, pour faciliter l'étude.*

Ce travail décrit comment important est l'utilisation de cet outil dans la science relativement nouvelle que l'archéologie subaquatique est, depuis l'emploi du SIG s'est étendu à des sous-disciplines de l'archéologie à tous les niveaux. Il est également prévu pour motiver d'autres archéologues pour en savoir plus à ce sujet, et l'utiliser dans de futurs projets.

Mots-clés: *SIG, Archéologie Sous-marine, Méthodologie*

INTRODUCTION

GIS is of greatly useful in all areas of archaeology. It supplies a spatial component to the more traditional database structures, allowing excellent acquisition, recording, analysis and visualization of geographic data.

Underwater Archaeology is a relatively young science, but increasingly the use of GIS within it has gained attention. In many ways its use in underwater archaeology is more complex than in land-based archaeology. Underwater archaeology needs a more careful strategy of management, research and conservation due to the impact both of nature and of the anthropogenic changes which are the result of coastal development and recreational activities.

Because of the relatively short periods of time available to recover material from the sea bed and the problems of being unfamiliar with a site in its totality due to poor visibility, GIS becomes especially important in underwater archaeological contexts.

It is easily seen that, because of the environment constraints, data is perceived on the surface as a whole. This is unlike what happens in land-based archaeology where interpretation begins in and is oriented towards fieldwork. Therefore this system is the best strategy available for the spatial analysis of an archaeological site since it allows easy input and output of cartographic information. In this way the whole context can be perceived or even restricted to a specific area. These changes in focus and perspective enhance our ability to interpret the archaeological record.

GIS APPLIED TO THE UNDERWATER ARCHAEOLOGY

Since the beginning of the use of computers in archaeology, the development of a tool that could provide software to manage the various digital formats has become indispensable.

Underwater excavations provide us with enough information to warrant the use of an efficient digital recording system. Before the use of GIS other digital recording systems such as the programme CAD were used. Nevertheless it was not possible to share data between them and it became necessary to learn how to use many different programs.

The first attempts in spatial analyses may have had their origin in the overlay of maps of a same area and with the same scale. These combined several thematic and spatial information features (Heywood et al., 2002: p. 176). With technological progress this manual process was transformed into a computerized format which consists of four components: hardware, software, geographic data and the human operator (ESRI, 1995).

The importance of spatial analysis in archaeology, especially at the inter-site level, is part of the postulates defended by the proponents of New Archaeology in the 1960s. There was a convergence of these ideas, at least at a theoretical level, in the development and use of Geographic Information Systems (Fontes, 2002). This resulted in what has come to be designated as 'the first phase of GIS' (Matos, 2001: p. 9).

The term was first applied by Roger Tomlinson in 1963 in his work on the CGIS Canada Geographic Information System. The following years were marked by the emergence of GIS software models (SyMAP, CALFORM, GRID, ODYSSEY). This was primarily focused on archaeological information work done using SyMap to analyze and calculate trend surfaces of archaeological sites (Wheatley *et al.*, 2002). In 1973, the University of Birmingham organized the first CAA international congress, which was dedicated to the theme of Computer Applications and Quantitative Methods in Archaeology. It came to set the foundations for the various national CAA congresses, including CAA Portugal (Figueiredo *et al.*, 2007). This congress contributed to the growing implementation of information systems in Archaeology, including the Geographic Information System. Also the book Spatial Analysis in Archaeology by Ian Hodder and Clive Orton, written in the 1970s, came up with a methodology to be used in the application of such systems in the interpretation of archaeological contexts.

In 1978, spatial analysis using GIS technology allowed researchers in southern Greece to carry out several survey studies which at once integrated the different levels of geomorphology and hydrology (Wheatley *et al.,* 2002: 18).

However, it was only in the 1980s that GIS began to be more widely used in archaeology in North America, with the application of predictive models in resource management (Burrought, 1986). Since then, the application of predictive models has frequently been used in numerous other countries (Djindjian, 1998), not only in the intra-sites analyses of site contexts (D'Andrea, 2003), but also in the inter-site relations between contexts. In the 1990s the use of GIS became more widespread, highlighting the increased use of predictive models. The first congress dedicated solely to the application of GIS to archaeology was held in Santa Barbara, California, in 1992; a subsequent one took place in Ravello, Italy, in 1993 (Lock *et al.*, 1995). The application of GIS to underwater archaeology however is more recent. It was first used in this century, notably in the UK, on important projects such as the Mary Rose shipwreck (from 1545), the Cattewater shipwreck (from 1550), in Plymouth Sound and in Breakwater Fort. It has also been used in the USA in projects under the auspices of the Institute of Nautical Archaeology in Texas. The first of those mentioned is one of the most famous projects in underwater archaeology. The wreck of Mary Rose, an English ship that sank off the coast of Portsmouth in 1545, was discovered in the 1960s and it was many years before an archaeological project took place. The excavation was documented within the Site Recorder software and the data and information about the findings and the structure of the wreck were added to a GIS in real time by means of an Acoustic Positioning System, as well as the details and descriptions provided by divers themselves (Holt, 2007). GIS gave the researchers a wider perspective on the data in this case and helped in the planning process (http://www.3hconsulting.com). The Cattewater site provides an instructive example of data processing in an underwater survey and excavation in which GIS allowed an accurate record. Due to these records, there could be a correlative analysis of the data obtained right from the beginning. The system was itself developed in Site Recorder 4 (SR4), which shares the basic functionalities of other GIS applications. This program also allowed recording of past events, giving an evolving perspective over time, integrating information from various campaigns of work done on site (Holt, 2007).

Also noteworthy is the work in GIS using *ArcInfo* and *ArcView* (ESRI) in Tel Shikmona, Haifa, Israel, on the Eastern Mediterranean coast, where remains from the Bronze Age (1500 BC) were first identified (Breman, 2003). These studies focused mainly on reconstructing the shoreline, on the demarcation of the commercial areas zones, on working out maritime and commercial routes, on the study of outside influences and contacts with other regions. These were evident from the examples of material culture from the Persian period (538 BC-332 BC) which they had discovered. In order to perform a more a detailed analysis of the data, geomorphologic, sedimentary and bathymetric characteristics were integrated into a GIS, along with the behaviours of currents and the coastal dynamics in Tel Shikmona. All of this contributed to providing unambiguous results, providing suitable explanations for the type of shipping and trade which was done at that time.

In parts of Scotland, Spain, and Italy GIS has come to be associated with the management and protection of underwater heritage. In Scotland a GIS-based platform aims to gather in one place all of the information available about known wrecks. This platform includes information about the type of work that has been carried out, as well the strategic plans that were at the beginning of this work, which is particularly useful for inter-site interpretation (Oxley, 2001).

A similar system was implemented in Andalusia. The Department of *Documentación, Formación y Diffusion*-IAPH of CAS (Centre for Archaeology *Subacuática del Instituto Andaluz de Patrimonio Histórico*) developed a spatial system to aid in the protection of underwater heritage on account of the large number of known shipwrecks in the coastal area; in the Bay of Cadiz alone there are over 870 documented cases of shipwrecks from the 15th through the 19th centuries (Alonso *et al.*, 2007).

The information system used, called ARQUEOS, possesses a geo-referenced database of known sites. It was linked to DOCUSUB, an information database of areas with potential findings, which performed searches based on documentary references in the historical archives. Later it came to incorporate findings that resulted from remote sensors and other detection instruments. This data was arranged in GIS in conjunction with information about environmental constraints and human exploitation such as the fishing industry, tourism and both public and private construction work. It contributed significantly to the protection and safeguarding of the remaining wrecks. Apart from this, the system is particularly useful in that it establishes a relationship between objects and factors such as tidal shifts, the dynamics of coastal winds, geomorphology, biological activity and others. It is used to develop predictive maps of the risk of these factors, which will then to be analyzed in order to create strategic plans to protect these areas.

Archeomar (http://www.archeomar.it/) designed by the Italian *Dipartimento per I Beni Culturali and Paesaggistici, Sezione per l'Archeologia Subacquea Technique* (Maritime Archaeology Section), a department in the Ministry of Cultural Heritage, is another example of the management and study of underwater heritage with a GIS application. It was created to allow recording, positioning and documenting works of value which lie underwater, off the coast of Campania, Basilicata, Puglia and Calabria.

All of this indicates that today GIS answers the needs of a fully integrated digital data management system in underwater archaeology (Matter and Wats, 2002). If it is to function as a new tool, GIS should meet certain requirements. It should be easier to learn; data should be displayed and read more simply; it should be easier to extract the information from this data; it should be sufficiently complex for a big project and sufficiently simple for a small project; it should allow the possibility of archiving and publishing information (Holt, on-line).

Thus GIS in underwater archaeology could allow the storage of information about an underwater site. As a tool it has the possibility of examining those morphological features that were introduced in the system, such as tides, winds, currents and sediment transport. It is also helpful in the assessment of coastal features, potential trade and shipwrecks of a site. All of this contributes to help the preservation of a site. Geophysical survey in an underwater project is a fine example of the usefulness of GIS. The results of geophysical surveying integrated with other data will permit the location and management of underwater findings.

GIS can also be used to study underwater landscapes in prehistoric periods. Because sea levels were lower in the glacial period, the analysis of those landscapes, now submerged, permit the reconstruction and definition of their outlines. The data collected can be placed into different layers in GIS, which can then either be shown or hidden on the map, permitting a user to see all kinds of information (Breman, 2003). The software is not limited to recording spatial data, it can also record temporal events by describing when things happened and their relationship to a site.

CONCLUSION

GIS is an important tool in the integration of multiple datasets and can modify the interpretation of traditional results of archaeological research. It can add information to existing approaches and supply additional opportuneties to study and analyze data.

GIS in underwater archaeology provides researchers with a useful tool to document information and to manage different data obtained during an investigation.

Data from different projects in underwater archaeological sites need GIS to help define possible areas of research. There are still many potential projects (many of which we know from oral sources) that need to embark on this tool in order to be studied and documented properly.

The versatility of GIS in the discipline of archaeology is better perceived by the combination with other sciences, for example with remote sensors. This multidisciplinary dimension and the reliance on other scientific disciplines will facilitate and result in an improvement in the quality of these projects. The main purposes of using GIS in underwater archaeology are the recognition of past landscapes, such as past coast line and settlements; identification of possible risk areas for wrecks; production of digital models of depth and contextualization of wrecks in their past landscapes.

GIS is a tool that permits the adjustment of historical elements with geographical components. In underwater archaeological projects, it can provide a single database that will integrate all of the gathered data, contribute to research activities and diffuse knowledge to the archaeological community.

References

ALONSO VILLALOBOS, Carlos; BENÍTEZ LÓPEZ, David; MÁRQUEZ CARMONA, Lourdes; VALIENTE ROMERO, Antonio; RAMOS MIGUÉLEZ, Silvia (SD) SIGNauta: un sistema para la información y gestión del património arqueológico subacuático de Andalucía.pdf [Consult. 20 de Fevereiro, 2012]. Also published in *PH Boletín del Instituto Andaluz del Patrimonio Histórico,* nº 63, agosto 2007, pp. 26-41. Available em: WWW:_URL:http://www.iaph.es/export/sites/default/galerías/arqueologiasubacuatica/documentos/xPDF-7x_SIGNauta.pdf_.

BENÍTEZ LÓPEZ, David; ALONSO VILLALOBOS, Carlos (SD) Aplicabilidad de los SIG para la gestión del património arqueológico subacuático andaluz:

SIGNauta.pdf. Available in WWW:_URL:http://www.iaph.es/export/sites/default/galerias/arqueologia-subacuatica/documentos/aplicabilidad_SIG_gestixn_PAS_SIGNAUTA.pdf_.

BREMAN, J. (2003) – Marine Archaeology goes Underwater with GIS. In *Journal of GIS in Archaeology*. Volume I. APRIL, 2003.

CHAPMAN, Henry (2006) – Landscape archaeology and GIS / Henry Chapman. – Stroud: Tempus.

CHURCH, T; BRANDON, R.J.; BURGETT, G.R. (2000) – GIS Applications in Archaeology: method in Search of Theory. In Westcott, K.L.; Brandon, R.J., eds., Practical Applications of GIS for Archaeologists: A predictive Modeling Kit, pp.135-155. London-Philadelphia: Taylor e Francis.

CROFF, Katherine (SD) – GIS and Underwater Archaeology.pdf Available in WWW:_URL:http://www.edc.uri.edu/nrs/classes/NRS409/509_2005/Croff.pdf_. [consult. 12 March 2012].

E.S.R.I. (1995) – *GIS in K-12 Education*, White Papers, Environmental Systems, Research Institute (E.S.R.I.): Redlands, Ca, USA, Available in WWW:_URLhttp://www.esri.com/library/journals/archaeology/volume_1/marine.pdf_. [consult. 20 March, 2012].

GILLINGS, M.; WISE, A. (1998) – GIS Guide to Good Practice. [Consult. 10 Fevereiro 2012]. Available in GIS Database: Available in WWW:_URL:http://ads.ahds.ac.uk/project/googguides/gis/_. [consult. 20 March, 2012].

HEYWOOD, I.; CORNELIUS, S,; CARVER, S. (2002) – An Introduction to Geographical Information Systems, 2ª Edição. Harçlow: Pearson education Limited.

HODDER. I.; ORTON, C. (1990) – Análisis Espacial en Arqueologia [ed. em Castelhano]. Barcelona: Editorial Crítica. [Consult. 10 Frebruary]. Available em: WWW:_URL:http://www.3hconsulting.com/_.

HOLT, Peter (2007) – Development of an Object-Oriented GIS for Maritime Archaeology – Motivation, Implementation and Results. in *Computer Applications and Quantitative Methods in Archaeology*. London: UK Chapter.

HOLT, Peter (2007) – The Use of GIS in Maritime Archaeology – the Cattewater Wreck Case Study, in *NAS Conference*. Available em: WWW:_URL:http://www.3hconsulting.com/Downloads/TheUseOfGISInMaritimeArchaeologyNAS2007.pdf_. [Consult. 20 March, 2012].

LOCK, G.; STANCIC, Z. (1995) – Archaeology and Geographical Information Systems, London. Bristol: Taylor and Francis.

MATHER, I.R.; G.P. WATTS. (2002) – Geographic information systems. In i*nternational Handbook of Underwater Archaeology*. C.V. Ruppe and J.F. Barstad, ed. New York: Kluwer Academic/Plenum Publishers. p. 679-696.

MATOS, J.L. (2001) – Fundamentos de Informação Geográfica. Lisboa: Libel.

MINISTERO PER I BENI E LE ATTIVITA' CULTURALI (Ministry of Cultural Heritage), Dipartimento per i Beni Culturali e Paesaggistici, *Sezione Tecnica per l'Archeologia Subacquea (Maritime Archaeology Section)* Progetto Archeomar. Available em http://www.archeomar.it/ [consult. no dia 23 de March de 2012].

OXLEY, I. (2001) – Towards the Integrated Management of Scotland's Cultural. Heritage: examining historic shipwrecks as marine environmental resources.

WHEATLEY, D.; GILLINGS, M. (2002) – Spatial Technology and Archaeology: The Archaeological Applications of GIS. London-New York: Taylor and Francis. World Archaeology. 32.3: p. 413-426.

MUSEALIZATION OF THE UNDERWATER HERITAGE OF THE WATERS OF SERGIPE

Ângela ANDRADE FERREIRA
Master in Archeology on the Graduation Program of the Federal University of Sergipe
angela_andrade1@hotmail.com

Elizabete de CASTRO MENDONÇA
Professor at Museology Department of the Federal University of Sergipe (NMS/ UFS); Coordinator of the Preventive Conservation Laboratory at the Museology Department of the Federal University of Sergipe (LABPREV/NMS/ UFS); Permanent MD of the Archeology Graduation Program of the Federal University of Sergipe (PROARQ-UFS)
elizabete.mendoca@gmail.com

Gilson RAMBELLI
Coordinator of the MD in Archeology Program (PROARQ-UFSermanent MD of the Anthropology Graduation Program of the Federal University of Sergipe. Coordinator of the Archeology Laboratory on the Underwater Environment Department of the Federal University of Sergipe (LAAA / NAR / UFS)
rambelli@arqueologiasubaquatica.org.br

Abstract: *This article has the intention to discuss the limits and possibilities of the underwater heritage musealization in the waters of Sergipe, as well as to analyze the potential of its possible communication process. This will work as an object of reflection of the feasibility of in situ preservation of underwater cultural heritage vessels Llyod Brasileiro Baependy, Araquara and Aníbal Benévolo, sunk during World War II, the German submarine Harro Schacht, also called U-507. Although the property in question has value and importance as a social, symbolic, emotional and political, the sinking of these ships were a gap to be filled regarding the history of Sergipe in Brazil and consequently. The theme relate the interface between Archaeology and Museology, so throughout this transit about theories related to both areas.*

Keywords: *Underwater Archaeology, Musealization, Underwater Cultural Heritage*

INTRODUCTION

This article has the intention to discuss the limits and possibilities of the underwater heritage musealization in the waters of Sergipe, as well as to analyze the potential of its possible communication process. As this paper relates the interface between Museology and Archeology, it seeks to emphasize the importance of the underwater heritage site towards its community, for that community can contribute to preserve that heritage for the future generations.

This project will work as an object of reflection of the feasibility of the application of underwater archeology techniques and *in situ* preservation of underwater cultural heritage vessels Llyod Brasileiro Baependy, Araquara and Aníbal Benévolo, sunk during World War II by the German submarine Harro Schacht, also called U-507. Although the property in question has social, symbolic, emotional and political value, the sinking of these ships is a gap to be filled, regarding the history of Sergipe and Brazil.

The vessels Llyod Brasileiro Baependy, Araquara and Aníbal Benévolo are still submerged and although searches have been made, they were not yet found. It is mandatory that research about this subject be conducted using archeological knowledge, which is a social science that allows the comprehension of the societies using cultural materials not only as objects, but also in an immaterial and symbolic dimension.

This underwater cultural heritage project should utilize not only bibliographic recourses, but also materials and testimonies. "Oral history can be faced as the history that one takes within". (Orser, 1992) On this perspective, the community insertion will take place since the initial stage of this research paper.

MUZEALIZATION

In a general approach, the musealization comprehends the selective value of the object. That valuation does not occur randomly, and does not have any specific environment to be held. It can occur through the guidance of the object within the museum or in situ in relation to material objects. It is worth noting that the musealization consists in a selective practice while exclusionary at the same time, since the object must have specifications to get its value and that some are valued over others. Before treating the museum object, it is necessary to understand what musealization is. Taking as starting point the text "O campo de atuação da museologia" from the author

Marília Xavier Cury, among many theorists cited by her, we will follow the musalization concepts determined by Waldisa Guarnieri, Cristina Bruno, Mario Chagas, and Marilia Cury herself. We chose to name them in chronological order to outline the changes over time and the "views" of each theorist on musealization. That does not necessarily means that one theory surpasses another, but that they are only different viewpoints.

In her definition, Waldisa Guarnieri says that "(...) musealization is much more than transfering object to the museum, because the act of musealization considers the information brought by the objects (sensu lato) in terms of documentation, testimonial, and fidelity" (...) (Guarnieri, 1990:8). It touches a point on the trajectory of the object inserted into the process of musealization now it is not considered a "utensil" to become a document. As an information carrier, the object does not explain himself, from the moment in which it "demonstrates" qualities as historicity, documentation, testimonial, authenticity, etc. that lead or justify its musealization. Ferrez based on Mensch says, "The object is the bearer of intrinsic information (deducted from the object itself) and extrinsic (obtained from sources other than the object) (Maciel, 2002:3), and this information coming from diverse sources, explained by qualities and with the contribution of the related fields of museology, will enable the construction of its history. What it is, how it is, how it is called, who made it, and having important relevance the context to which the object was previously inserted.

The definition presented by Cristina Bruno understands musealization as, "(...) the set of procedures that enables the communication of interpreted objects (research results) to interpreting views (public) within the museum institutions (...)" (Bruno, 1991:17). It gives importance, to a certain extent, to the technical part (practical procedures) of musealization stating that, "(...) It is a set of procedures", treating musealization as a process, which its integral parts – research, conservation, and documentation, serve as pillars to achieve its final objective. That objective is the communication, to the public, of objects that have already been submitted to the process and that bring information from the research conducted for the occurrence of an institutionalization to the public – the great motivator of completing the process musealization to a given object. It is noteworthy that the process does not end at the time the public has contact with the object. From the events and/or reactions from the public in contact with the object, there is a restart of actions toward the object, since the musealization process consists on cyclical actions linked to the dynamics, which the object is submitted or entered.

Mario Chagas defines the power exerted by the museologist about the destination and value of each object through said "museoalgcal view". This view is not neutral. It is filled with ideologies, among other issues, which will serve as guidelines of the options and decisions taken by the museologist. According to Chagas: "The musealization is a process that begins with the selection made by the "museological view" on material things, i.e. "(...) a critical and questioning attitude, capable of a reflective distance from the set of cultural and natural materials (...)". (Chagas, 1996, 99). It is noteworthy that on the premise that there is no science and therefore neutral scientist, their conceptions as individuals also conducted interference and inference on their professional attitude toward the objects.

Marilia Cury understands musealization as "(...), the valuation of objects. (...). The musealization, then, starts on the selective valuation, but remains in the set of actions aimed at transforming the object into a document and its communication." (Cury, 2005:24). Understanding the valuation as a starting point, the musealization does not end at this stage, highlighting the importance of other steps that are of great importance in the transition from "object utensil" to "document object", the product of research conducted in the musealization process, which will provide its communication to the scientific public or not.

In this perspective, it is necessary that the musealized object do not be treated isolated towards building the relationship with its social context. It is of paramount importance to relate it, as it belongs to the social contexts of the past, present and future. In order to perform the contextualization it is important to communicate the meaning of this heritage within the context in which it appears, giving priority to the community in which it was and/or is inserted. Considering that the process of musealization is not a streamlined process for preservation and subsequent communication although it is cyclic, it has steps that are crucial to its initiation and success. The first step is the acquisition, which is "the beginning" or "starting point", because in "possession" of the given object the remaining steps will begin. The second step is the research, which will fetch the intrinsic and extrinsic information to the object held in parallel to the procedures of conservation and documentation. The third and final step is the communication process, which will be responsible for the dissemination of the object through the means available for its provision and extroversion, as well as knowledge produced in the academic and extra academic environment.

UNDERWATER HERITAGE COMMUNICATION: THE PRODUCT OF MUSEALIZATION

In Brazil, a major problem, which turns out to be the precursor of other Maritime and Underwater Archaeology problems, is the lack of knowledge of the existence of underwater heritage by the community. CEANS/SEN evaluates that the disrespect and depredation of underwater cultural heritage, especially on shipwrecks, are due largely to lack of knowledge and misinformation. (Livro Amarelo, 2004, p. 2). This problem, which may be solved as soon as the product of research, being archaeological or from other areas that have the same focus, is released to the scope of the community. The underwater cultural heritage brought a new dilemma for heritage discussions, since the preservation and conservation of this *extra situ* is quite costly and exposes the object to a considerable degradation. Taking into account that in the first moment the object is removed from the underwater environment and maintains contact with the air the degradation process starts, the in situ preservation and the heritage sustainability have been the two subjects of discussions. However, it should be noted that an exacerbated preservation will further separate an audience that do not even have knowledge of what it is or what is the significance of that heritage, what would lead to the degradation of its structure. In submitting the object to a sustainability system, it would become accessible to the community, which would lead it to an exhibition of large proportion. It is important to emphasize that the sustainability issue is not about remnant unregulated commercial exploitation of the remains of shipwrecks held in the past that led to physical and documental deterioration. Based on studies, it seeks to integrate the heritage object with the community and, as far as possible, to make it self-sustaining, which will provide funds for its autonomy with regard to the preservation and conservation. The underwater archaeological vestige cannot be reduced to a mere informative function and knowledge in face of its "survival" needs and testimony to contemporary and future societies.

In Brazil, as occurred elsewhere in the world, the shipwreck Archaeology, which represents the integration of archaeological specialties such as navigation (the vessel), the underwater (the site environment), and maritime (the society) in a specific category of an archaeological site (Rambelli, 2006:98), suffered marginalization within the academic world. This resulted in the difficulty encountered by researchers in this field to initiate or progress on their research. Because there is this internal segregation in Archaeology, archaeological sites of shipwrecks became more susceptible to violation and disrespect, either by local collectors of floating remnants of the sunken vessels or by treasure hunters inspired by the legend of submerged fortunes. These, for some time, has been easy targets for diving treasure hunters, who are not linked to the principles or laws relating to archeology or underwater archeology.

According to Funari & Pellegrini (2006, p. 28):

> "The looting of shipwrecks – with their loads with commercial value, already alerted to the seriousness of the problem of ownership of commercial heritage, since it loses, in this case, the whole context that can give meaning to underwater objects taken by underwater piracy."

These explorers became present in the Brazilian coast after being banned from international waters. Since they could not loot the submerged heritage located in other parts of the world, they focused in Brazil. Here, they found a free territory for exploration and without interference to the achievement of looting – the artifacts collected here were transferred to collectors and museums, based on the prerogative that once submerged, things are lost and belong to those who find them. Given this situation, it was determined that 80% of the artifacts "rescued" would belong to the explorer and 20% would be ownership of the Brazilian government, according to the text of the Federal Law 7.542/86.

Transposing to the international legal foundations of underwater cultural heritage, we quote the text of the 31st General Conference of the United Nations Organization for Education, Science and Culture (UNESCO) by ICUCH – International Committee on Underwater Cultural Heritage. That is an example of how international law are manifested about preservation *in situ,* as well as the inclusion of the community in the process of preservation and conservation of cultural heritage, specifically underwater heritage. According to the official text, titled Convention on the Protection of Underwater Cultural Heritage, Paris, 2001, article II, 5th, 6th and 7th paragraphs, providing the input for interaction with the community, as it is preserved *in situ*, the object must inform the community in which is inserted with priority.

5. The preservation *in situ* of underwater cultural heritage shall be considered as the first option before allowing or initiating any activity directed at this cultural heritage.

6. The recovered underwater cultural heritage shall be deposited, conserved and managed in a way that ensures its long-term preservation.

7. The underwater cultural heritage shall not be subject to commercial exploitation.

The new position of archaeological research based on paragraph 5 is related to a problem that today's Archaeology Museums face, which is the over-collection due to excessive drilling without taking in consideration whether the museums have the infrastructure to hold all of the artifacts collected with premised on the preservation, conservation and consequently their communication. In the case of artifacts submerged when collected, since it remained immersed in the environment for a prolonged period, when brought to the surface will suffer various "degradations" related to the change of environment, becoming burdensome its preservation and maintenance in general. Exceptionally, they can be removed, by expert assessment, from the submerged environmental in equilibrium with it. If "warehoused" in technical reserve and isolated from the public, it will not fulfill its social role, because the vast collection prevents the execution of all steps relevant to the process of musealization.

Faced with the unviability of existing museums of receiving new artifacts, either in technical reserves or in exhibition areas, due to the limited physical and financial infrastructure, increasingly becomes pertinent the musealization *in situ*. That will provide targeted interventions on the site without degrading the same and its constituent parts, and the creation of virtual exhibition spaces that allow the dialogue between the individual and the underwater cultural heritage, as well as enable future generations to carry the same interpretations based on the context of their time.

> "Hence the importance of giving prestige or legal apparatus that enables the conservation of the archaeological site and its context (or its recovery and research) for later production of knowledge, with more advanced technologies, and probably with more profound and mature academic discussions. At the same time, the maintenance of archaeological basis for in situ conservation means enabling the interregnum time required for deliberation, which connects the principle to one of the foundations of the environmental principle of precaution (...)." (Soares, 2007:98).

The Federal Law 7.542/86, determines the Union as the owner of submerged archaeological sites, being responsible for the protection and exploitation of the submerged cultural heritage the Navy of Brazil, not being mentioned the Institute of Historical and Artistic Heritage (IPHAN), the federal agency that has the task of safeguarding the historical, artistic and cultural heritage. This measure confirmed this stance in maintaining this vision of the underwater cultural heritage, relegating it to exoticism and being treated as something that neither falls within what is understood as property, nor is valued, so not getting due recognition.

If the underwater heritage was subjected to the liability of the IPHAN federal agency and other bodies related to the preservation and safeguarding of assets, or a body that offered specific treatment for this property was created, as recommended by the international laws, actions of conservation, preservation, and outreach would already have being implemented. Using cultural heritage education tools, it could effectively promote it among the population. This dialogue between Archaeology and education was named the Public Archaeology:

Archaeology with the public or Public Archaeology, arouse decades ago as a set of actions and reflections that aimed to know to whom the knowledge produced by archeology is interesting, how its research affects society, and how it is being presented to the public. More than one line of research within the discipline, the Public Archaeology is inherent to the application of the profession. (Heifer Almeida, 2002; Funari, 2002. & Heifer In da Silveira, 2007, p. 85).

According to Funari, "(...) the creation of an identity depends on the preservation of places with their evocations of our memory." (Funari, 2010). Therefore, for the local community to contribute to the preservation of the cultural heritage, first it is necessary to perform actions to ascertain the awareness of the value of the cultural heritage, clarifying what is necessarily this cultural heritage in question and how it comes to be part of its own history. The history of a nation is the history of each individual who may dwell in your geographic territory thus generating the identification of the individual, which will result in the preservation its history.

An important point in the preservation of underwater heritage refers to the fact that local legislation goes in opposite direction to international laws that treat the specifics of submerged archaeological heritage. The international laws were created in order to preserve and safeguard the underwater cultural heritage. The national law 10,166/00 had a preponderant role in the depredation of this heritage, as it defines it as "things and possessions of artistic, historic or archaeological interest", offering support to undue exploitation and trade of goods originating from archaeological sites formed from sunken vessels (shipwrecks sites). For treating underwater cultural heritage artifacts as valuables properties, it conceives intrusive intervention on this heritage as a simple operation to recover objects from the bottom of the sea, especially the remains of sunken ships. (Rambelli, 2009).

It is important nowadays to search for improvements regarding the laws and knowledge on the subject, as well as the training of new professionals to work in underwater archeology in Brazil. In specific, in Sergipe, because it's known that there is a submerged unexplored heritage on the coast of Sergipe that needs to go through an inventory process in order to be diffused, as well as avoiding the subtraction of their constituent parts.

CONSIDERATIONS

The act of previously recovering the underwater cultural heritage from the environmental and safeguard it in institutions enables the management and dissemination to the community, undermining the commercial exploitation by the treasure hunters. Thus, archeology cannot be thought without reference to museology, the study of heritage management, and its public aspect. (Funari, 2010) Making musealization *in situ* is an increasingly relevant and proper posture, promoting the Underwater Archaeology – while science, deconstructing the view of whether it is an adventurous activity and the demystificating the elitist character which is assigned to it.

Analyzing the information on the national scene for the underwater archaeological heritage, it is apparent that the problems faced by it have their origin in the lack of knowledge of its existence by the community. Taking in consideration the fact that the disrespect and damaging of this heritage are caused by the lack of knowledge and information, it becomes necessary the musealization of the underwater heritage, subjecting it to a process of communication, research, and consequent protection that best fit its situation. Furthermore, comprising both as integral parts of the musealization process to be held from research relating to the heritage in question and with actions with and for the community in order to insert it in the contemporary culture. It is worth mentioning that for this cultural heritage to fulfill its social function in a broad and effective way, it is necessary to give it proper visibility. It is important that the research on underwater cultural heritage in the interface of Museology with

Archaeology, focus on the information produced from the possibilities, strategies, methods and procedures necessary to the extraversion of this archaeological heritage to the population in an extra academic sphere so that it can contribute with regard to the preservation and conservation of it.

References

BLOT, Jean-Yves (1999) – "O mar de Keith Muckelroy: o papel da teoria na arqueologia do mundo náutico". *Al-Madan*, Almada, Centro de Arqueologia, Série 2, n. 8, pp. 41-55.

BRUNO, Maria Cristina Oliveira (1995) – Musealização da Arqueologia: um estudo de modelos para o Projeto Paranapanema. São Paulo: FFLCH – USP.

CONVENTION ON THE PROTECTION OF THE UNDERWATER CULTURAL HERITAGE. Text adopted by the 31th General Conference of the United Nations Organization in Education, Science and Culture (UNESCO) in Paris on November 2, 2001. Translation of Francisco J.S. Alves (Director of the National Center for Maritime and Underwater Archaeology of the Portuguese Institute of Archaeology) made from the original versions in English, French and Spanish. Adaptation (unofficial) to the Portuguese of Brazil Gilson Rambelli. [Consult. 28 de Fev. 2010]. Disponível em http://www.arqueologiasubaquatica.org.br/downloads/index.html_.

CURADORIA MUSEOLÓGICA. Museologia. (2008) – Caderno de diretrizes museológicas 2, Belo Horizonte: Secretaria de Estado da Cultura, Superintendência de Museus.

CURY, Marília Xavier (2008) – Exposição – Concepção, montagem e avaliação. 2ª. ed. São Paulo, Annablume.

DIEGUES, A.C. (1998) – Ilhas e mares: simbolismo e imaginário. São Paulo: Hucitec.

FILHO, Manuel Ferreira Lima; ECKERT, Cornelia; BELTRÃO, Jane (2007) - Antropologia e Patrimônio Cultural. Diálogos e Desafios Contemporâneos. Blumenau: Nova Letra.

FUNARI, Pedro Paulo (2007) – Arqueologia e patrimônio. Erechim: Habilis.

FUNARI, Pedro Paulo (2010) – Arqueologia. São Paulo: Contexto.

FUNARI, Pedro Paulo; PELEGRINI, Sandra C.A. (2006) – Patrimônio Histórico e Cultural. Rio de Janeiro: Jorge Zahar Editor, (Passo-a-Passo).

GONÇALVES, José Reginaldo (2007) – Monumentalidade e cotidiano: os patrimônios culturais como gênero de discurso. In: Gonçalves, José Reginaldo. Antropologia dos objetos: coleções, museus e patrimônios – Rio de Janeiro: IPHAN: Garamond, p. 139-158. (Coleção museu, memória e cidadania, v. 2).

LIVRO AMARELO: MANIFESTO PRÓ-PATRIMÔNIO CULTURAL SUBAQUÁTICO BRASILEIRO. CAMPINAS, JUNHO DE 2004 CEANS / NEE / UNICAMP – [Consult. 28 de Fev. 2010]. Disponível em:www:_URL:http//:www.unicamp.br/nee/arqueologia_.

MACHADO, Neli T. Galarce; LOPES, Sérgio Nunes; GHENO, Diego Antônio (2009) – Arqueologia Histórica e a problemática do patrimônio: discussões acerca da preservação, turismo e educação patrimonial no Vale do Taquari – Rio Grande do Sul. História, vol. 28, no. 1, Franca.

NAVIGATOR: (2006) – Subsídios para a história marítima do Brasil, v. 2, n.4. Rio de Janeiro: Serviço de Documentação da Marinha.

NETTO, Carlos Xavier De Azevedo (2008) – Preservação do patrimônio arqueológico – reflexões através do registro e transferência da informação. Ci. Inf., vol. 37, no. 3, Brasília, Sept./Dec.

ORSER, C.E. (1992) – Introdução à Arqueologia Histórica. Belo Horizonte, Oficina de Livros.

PELEGRINI, Sandra C.A., Org.; RAMBELLI, Gilson (2009) – Org. Patrimônio Cultural e Ambiental: questões legais e conceituais. São Paulo: Annablume; FAPESP, Campinas: Nepam.

RAMBELLI, Gilson (2007) – Preservação sob as ondas – A proteção do patrimônio subaquático brasileiro – Revista do Patrimônio Histórico e Artístico Nacional, v. 1, p. 136-151.

RAMBELLI, Gilson (2003) – Arqueologia até debaixo d'água. São Paulo: Maranta.

RAMBELLI, Gilson (2006) – Arqueologia de naufrágios e a proposta de estudo de um navio negreiro. Revista de História da Arte e Arqueologia, v. 6, p. 97-106.

RAMBELLI, Gilson (2008) – Entre o uso social e o abuso comercial: as percepções do patrimônio cultural subaquático no Brasil. História, vol. 27, no. 2, Franca.

RAMBELLI, Gilson (2010) Patrimônio cultural subaquático no Brasil: Discrepâncias conceituais, incongruência legal. In. Funari, Pedro Paulo A, Org.

RAMBELLI, Gilson (2004) – Os desafios da Arqueologia Subaquática no Brasil. Revista eletrônica História e-História. [Consult. 09 de Out. 2010]. Disponível em www:_URL:http://www.historiaehistoria.com.br_.

RAMBELLI, Gilson (2006) – Tráfico e navios negreiros: contribuição da Arqueologia Náutica e Subaquática. Navigator: subsídios para a história marítima do Brasil, v. 2, p. 59-72.

RAMBELLI, Gilson & FUNARI, P.P.A. (2007) – Los desafíos del patrimonio arqueológico subacuático en Brasil: pensamientos varios. Memorias: Revista Digital de Historia y Arqueología desde el Caribe. Universidad del Norte, (14 p.). [Consult. 11 de Out. de 2010]. Disponível em: www:_URL:http://www.uninorte.edu.co/publicaciones/memorias/memorias_7/articulos/rambellifunari.pdf_.

SANTACANA MESTRE, Joan; SERRAT ANTOLÍ, Núria (Coord.) (2005) – Museografía didáctica. Barcelona: Ariel.

SALADINO, Alejandra. Arqueologia patrimonializada e desenvolvimento social: perspectivas no Brasil e em Portugal. (2009) [Consult. 08 de Out. 2010]. Disponivel em: www:_URL:http://revistamuseologiaepatrimonio.mast.br/index.php/ppgpmus/article/viewFile/58/72_.

SANTOS, Myrian Sepúlveda dos (Org.) (2007) – Museus, coleções e patrimônios: narrativas polifônicas. Rio de Janeiro: IPHAN: Garamond, p. 229-245. (Coleção museu, memória e cidadania).

TRIGGER, B.G. (2004) – História do pensamento arqueológico. (trad. Ordep Trindade Serra). São Paulo: Odysseus.

PRIMO, Judite (1999) – Museologia e Património: Documentos Fundamentais. São Paulo: FFLCH – USP.

SOARES, Inês Virgínia Prado (2007) – Proteção jurídica do patrimônio arqueológico no Brasil: fundamentos para efetividade da tutela em face de obras e atividades impactantes. Erechim: Habilis, 228 p.

SOUZA FILHO, C Arlos Frederico Marés de (2009) – Bens culturais e sua proteção jurídica. 3ª Ed. (ano 2005), 5ª tir. Curitiba: Juruá.

CAVE BACELINHO, ALVAIÁZERE – FROM SANTOS ROCHA TO THE NEW INVESTIGATIONS: THE CONSERVATION OF ARCHAEOLOGICAL IRON ARTEFACTS

Alexandra FIGUEIREDO
Professor in Instituto Politécnico de Tomar
alexfiga@ipt.pt

Cláudio MONTEIRO
Doctoral student in Trás-os-Montes and Alto Douro University & Polytechnic Institute of Tomar
claudio.monteiro.cr@gmail.com

Helena FÉLIX
Polytechnic Institute of Tomar
helenafelix@ipt.pt

Abstract: *The cave of Bacelinho is located in central Portugal, in the region of Alvaiázere. This is apparently a artificial cavity, originally excavated by the Romans for the mineral extraction. In the archaeological interventions carried out were exhumed several metal objects from the various timelines. This cavity is extremely wet and has very specific environmental characteristics which reflected in the conservation of archaeological objects and raised a number of questions regarding to the process of degradation of metals. These articles have the aim to expose these singularities, trying to relate them with the surrounding environment and the actual archaeological context.*

Key-words: *Cave; Metals preservation; Iron; Underwater Archaeology*

Résumé: *La grotte de Bacelinho est situé dans le centre du Portugal, dans la région de Alvaiázere. C'est apparemment une cavité artificielle, creusée à l'origine par les Romains pour l'extraction du minerai de fer et de rester à l'occupation occupations sporadiques au cours du temps. Dans les interventions archéologiques réalisées à ce jour, ont été exhumés de plusieurs objets métalliques des échéances diverses. Cette cavité est extrêmement humide et a caractéristiques environnementales spécifiques, qui ont été reflétées dans la conservation des objets archéologiques, a soulevé un certain nombre de questions relatives au processus de dégradation des métaux et leur intégration dans le cadre méthodologique de l'archéologie sous-marine. Cet article se propose d'exposer brièvement ces singularités, en essayant de les mettre en relation avec l'environnement et le contexte archéologique.*

Mon-clé: *Cave; La preservation des métaux; Fer; Archaéologie sous-marine*

Resumo: *A gruta do Bacelinho localiza-se no centro de Portugal, concelho de Alvaiázere, distrito de Leiria. Trata-se de uma cavidade aparentemente semiartificial, aberta no período clássico para a extração de minério e apresentando ocupações esporádicas ao longo dos tempos. Nos inícios do século XX, Santos Rocha, chamado a atenção por um dos habitantes, deu-lhe destaque pela intervenção de duas sondagens, tendo-a reconhecido como uma mina luso-romana (1853-1910). Somente após um século o sítio foi revisitado para dar lugar a um trabalho mais persistente. Nas intervenções arqueológicas levadas a cabo foram exumados vários objetos metálicos, provenientes das várias fases de ocupação. O fato desta cavidade ser extremamente húmida e possuir características ambientais muito específicas, que se refletiram na conservação dos objetos arqueológicos, levantou uma série de questões relativas ao processo de degradação dos metais e a sua integração metodológica conservativa no âmbito da arqueologia subaquática. Este artigo pretende expor resumidamente estas singularidades, tentando relaciona-las com o ambiente envolvente e o contexto arqueológico.*

Palavras chave: *Gruta, Conservação de metais, Ferro, Arqueologia subaquática*

ENVIRONMENTAL CONTEXT

The place is a mine where the limestone is composed of iron oxide, given the cave reddish tinge. This factor, coupled with the fact of this cave being too wet, becomes the environment particularly interesting from the point of view of conservation of ferrous metals.

It must be pointed out that in these types of excavations, because of the environment, they should be treated with methodologies that fit the theoretical and practical concepts of underwater archeology and conservation. So, the lack of understanding and use of these methods may result in the total destruction of the remains.

THE ARCHAEOLOGICAL PLACE

The Bacelinho Cave is composed of a wide space, arranged in three main halls and several galleries attached

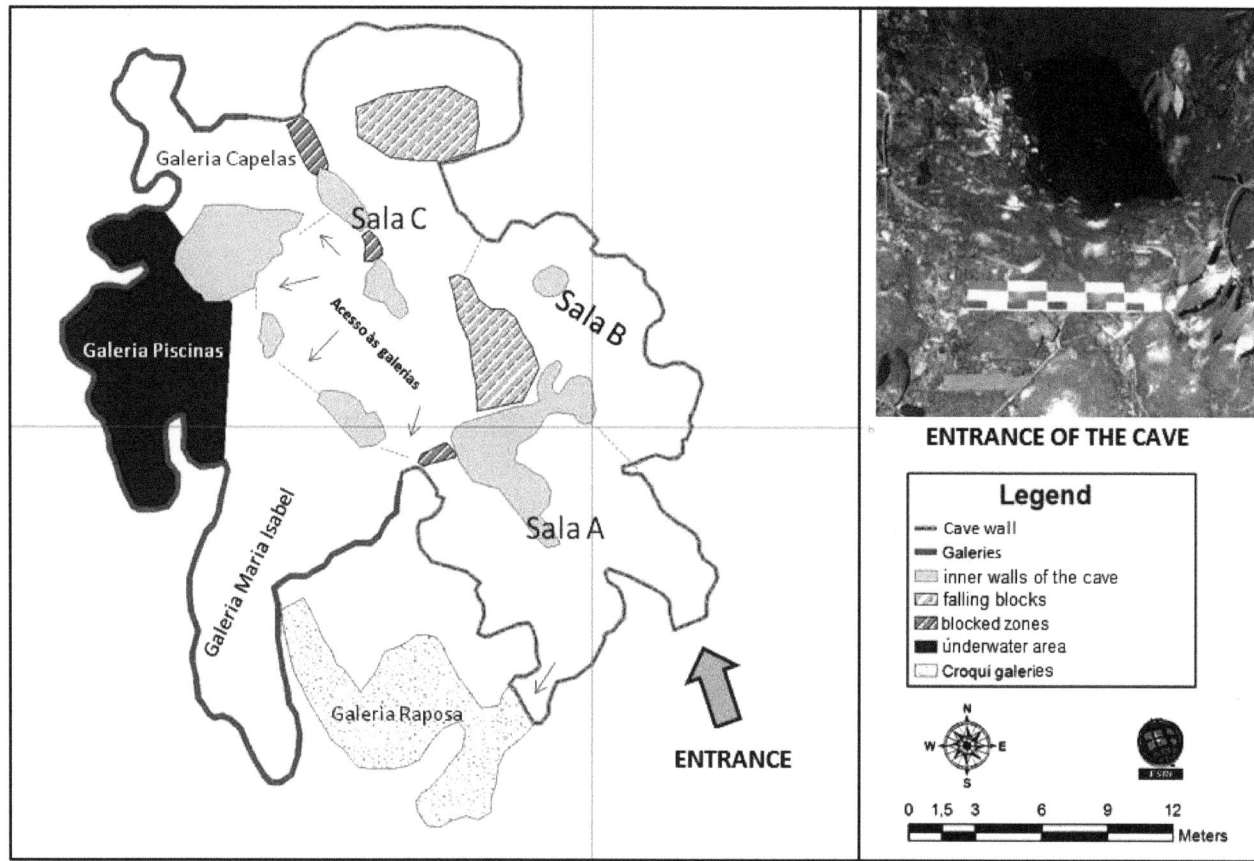

Figure 1 – General plan of the cave showing the entrance area of the cavity, enclosed rooms and galleries

with a total size of more than 500 square meters. The internal environment has high moisture content, always over 90%. The soil is mostly silty, having two galleries completely submerged, with a depth that reaches 50 cm in winters. The entrance is relatively narrow, about 60 cm wide, facing south (figure 1).

Most rooms have signs of mining extraction. The main rooms were named Sala A, B and C and the galleries had a name as the features observed, like Fox Gallery (Galeria da Raposa), Maria Isabel (Galeria Maria Isabel), Pools (Galeria das Piscinas) and Chapels (Galeria das Capelas).

In all of them were checked material traces of the classical period. However, the observed higher percentage of artefacts recorded to the first room (sala A), led us to invest and focus our study in this area, during the year 2011, being from this space all the objects presented here.

This room had a set of stone structures that have the probably function of delimiting spaces, composed, in the upper zone, of a possible stakes or wooden planking, which supported a roof, in some places, made by *tegula* and *imbrex*. In these insides spaces we exhumed a lot of coals.

If we consider the moist environment in question, these roof structures serve to filter the water droplets fall observed on the walls and in the ceiling of the cavity.

In the zone further south we note a fireplace with a diameter greater than 1.20 cm and bordered by small stones. This fireplace has about 30 cm tall and is strategically positioned, getting the currents air that having access from the Fox gallery, which has also a small slit in contact with the outside, the southeast wall. This feature creates a small flow of air between the room A and the gallery, allowing the combustion and heat maintenance and the removal of carbon monoxide from the cavity, preventing intoxication.

Associated to the stone structures we recovered a wide variety of ceramic fragments, some in *sigilata*; fragments of glass containers, two flints, three natural crystals quartz and a number of metal objects that integrate between the Romans and medieval times (figure 3).

It was recovered more than thrity iron objects.

It was also exhumed a diversity of wildlife, especially the *sus scrofa*, *cervidae*, *ovis/capra* and some *ave* and *carnivora*.

This article aims, however, limit itself to the conservation treatment of the iron metals and analysis of particular pathologies recorded, with special emphasis on objects integrated in the classical period (II and III century AD).

From this time about the iron artefacts we highlight some fasteners, working mining (like iron wedge) and Roman

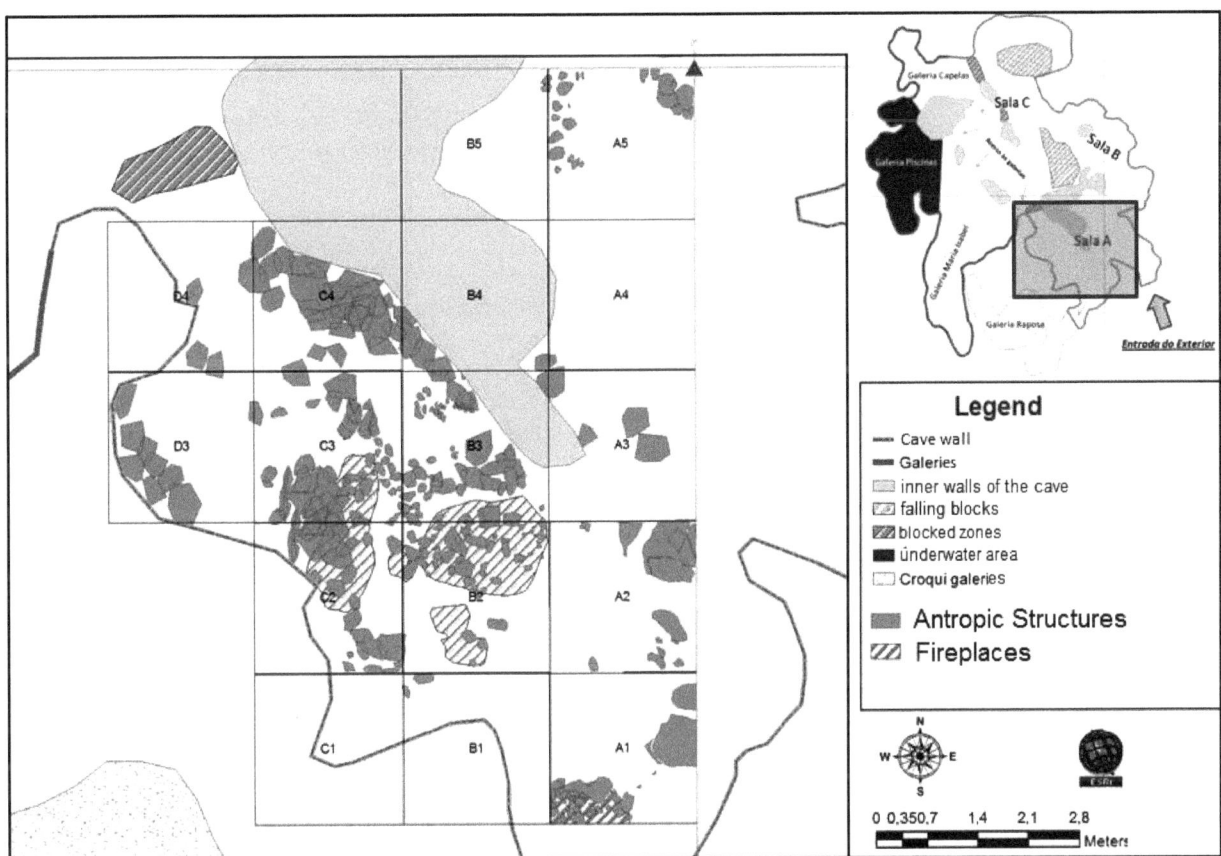

Figure 2 – The room layout with the detail of the stone structures, concentrating zone coals (squares B and C) and fireplace (grid A1)

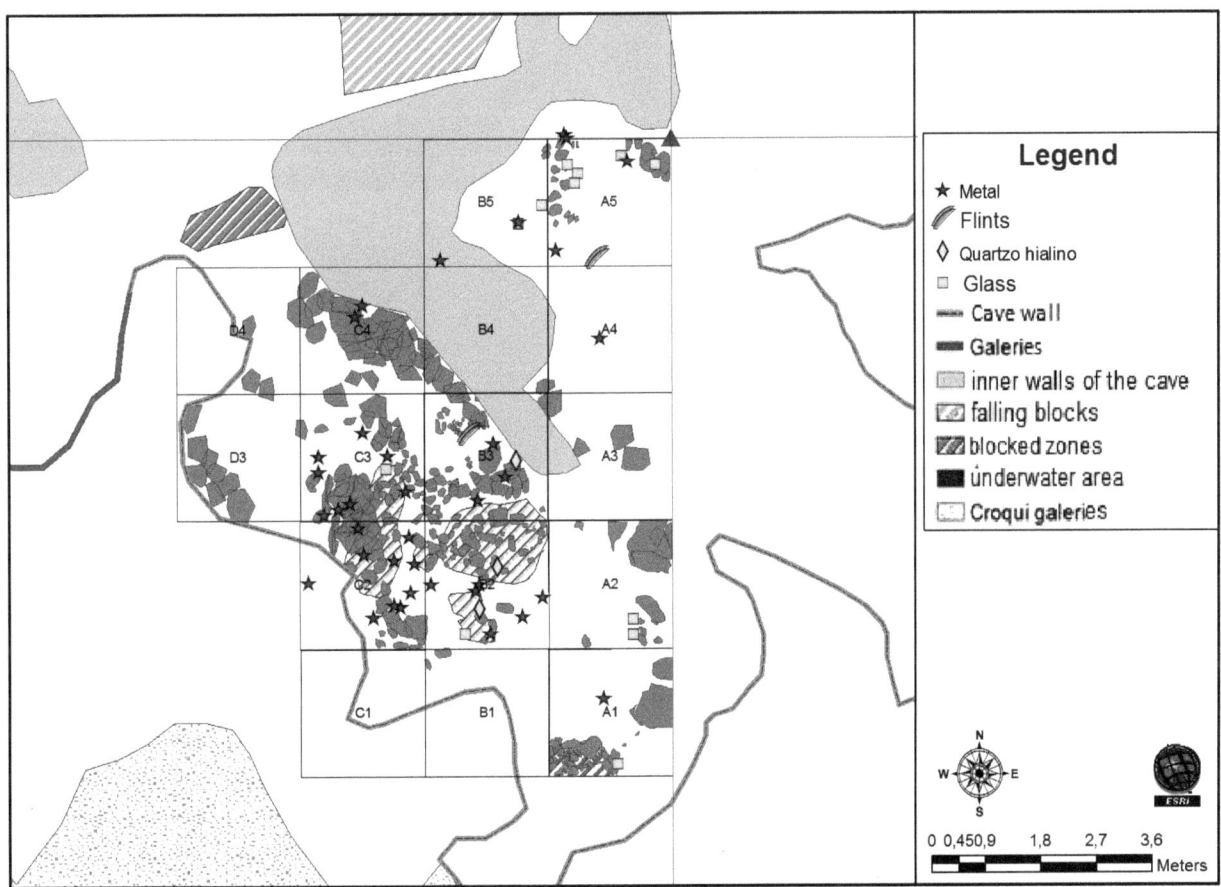

Figure 3 – Excavated area with the spatial representation of the elements of glass, metal and lithic

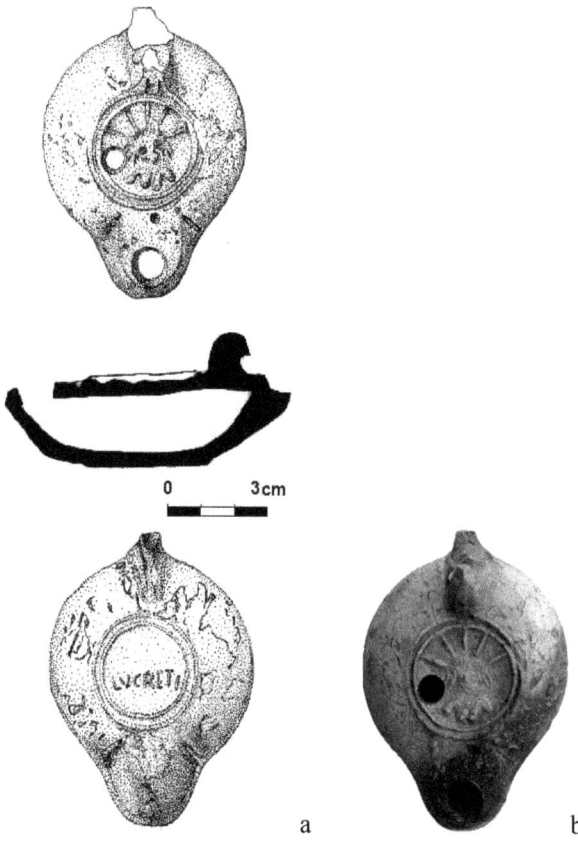

weaponry (arrowhead, spearhead, two swords and various *pilum*).

Among the elements that allow us to assess this chronology we include one Lucerne dedicated to Helios (the Sun God), with signs of use and possession of a small inscription on the base [LUCRECI] founded in the same level of this iron artefacts.

The different layers reported, considering that we are in a room with a sediment deposition traced by the entry run, are hardly noticeable. However it was considered two general stratigraphic levels, being the lowest the level that have the classical remains.

The metal objects are mostly spatially concentrated at the center of the room (squares C2, B2, B3 and C3), near of one roof abatement zone (considered by the presence of very fragments of *tegula* and *imbrex*) and concentration of carbon (derived probably from the destruction of the perishable structure that support the roof). It is noticeable especially the metal elements considered fastening founded around these patches of coal.

The swords are located in close proximity to one another. It is also noted that the sword from the grid C3 was registered under a *tegula* and both are integers.

Figure 4 – Drawing (a) and photo of Lucerne (b) (II and III century AD).

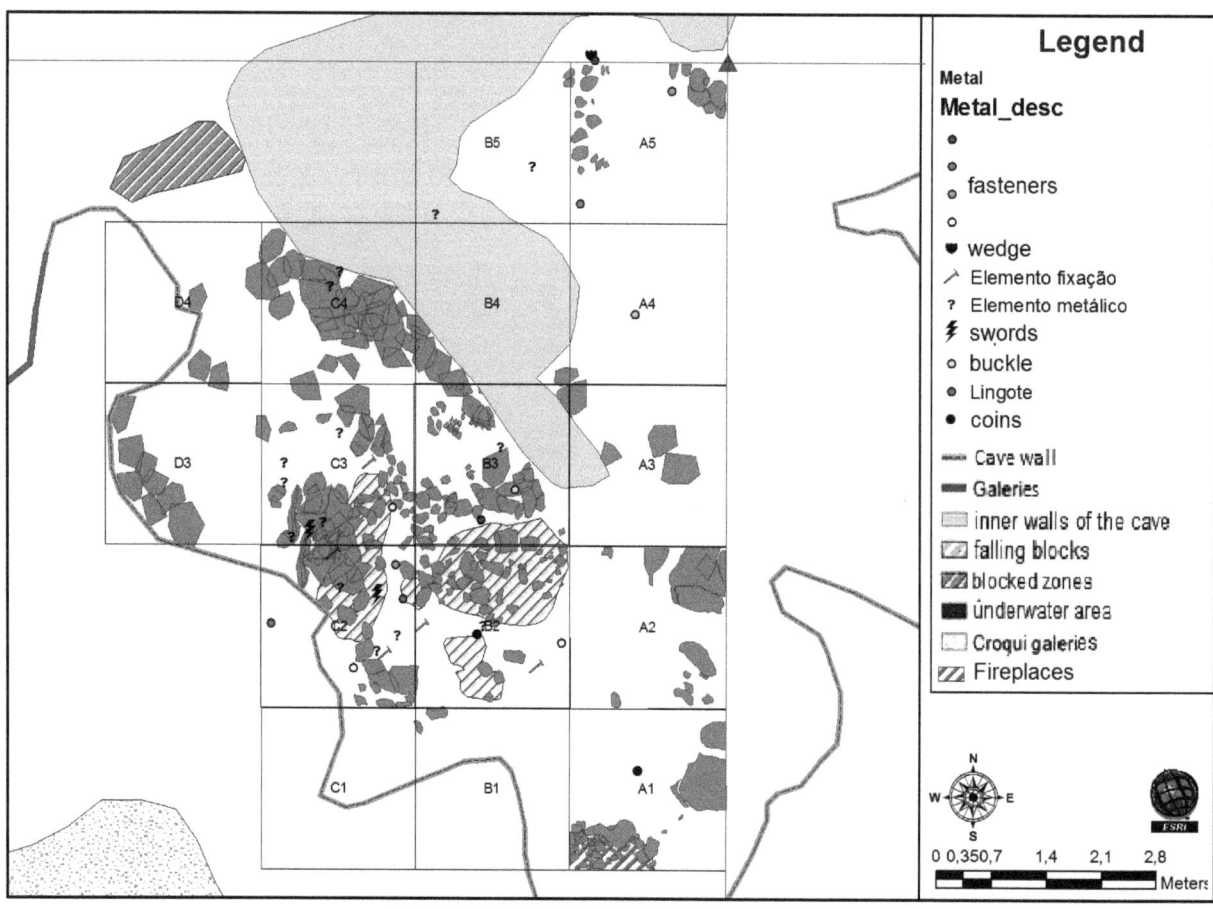

Figure 5 – The room layout indicating the squares and metal artifacts recovered

METALS AND THEIR STATE OF CONSERVATION

Overall, almost all objects exhumed were very weak. The oldest layers showed large concretion, comprising iron oxides and scale of local rock.

The metals in general, but especially recorded in C and D squares bearing an abnormal condition where seemingly contrary to what is expected, there has been an iron deposit on the surface of the objects. Yet, despite this increase metal, the core was very weak. A concrete example of this situation is shown by swords, wherein the blade should not have more than 5mm thick, with variations in regions had 1 to 2 cm thick.

This increase in volume corresponds to no oxidation or layers of concretions in normal media objects from moist, but molten metal (figure 6) contrasting with the interior weak. The cause of this pathology is still unclear, however, consider that these objects have been accidentally exposed to high temperatures and, in this sense, some of the ore in this cave blew up, adding to the objects, then suffering deteorization by corrosion. This factor is supported by the high number of existing coal near the place where they were exhumed, and we can put in this case the hypothesis of a strong fire where focus structures already described.

Figure 6 – Detail of sword treated, which is visible the uneven caused by the increase of metal

Figure 7 – Wedge, after clean, where you can observe the deformation and small superficial blisters

Figure 8 – Arrowhead, after clean, where we can observe the small superficial blisters

Alongside this, it is still noteworthy, the type of corrosion. This is due to corrosion by bubbling hydrogen concentrations, one type of rare observation, creating deformations and very irregular appearance to the metal surface, resembling blistering or bubbling on the surface (figure 7 and 8). In the level of conservation, this disease causes inside crackers, leaving the metal very brittle (Eliaz *et al.*, 2002).

TREATMENT OF CONSERVATION

The treatments were based on the assessment of the conservation status of the metals, and based on the procedures used in the laboratory of Archaeology and Conservation of Submerged Heritage of Polytechnic Institute of Tomar (Portugal).

The intervention was based on three phases:

1. Cleaning – careful removal of layers of concretion. Were not removed the increments metal, except in one of the Roman swords, which, due to size and heavy weight of the increment was necessary to cut, using the grinder, part of the excess metal in order to restore balance and stability to the workpiece.

2. Stabilization – tempering treatment at high temperatures for removal of chlorides. The choice of this treatment is due to the fact that is a rapid and very effective method in eliminating them (Hamilton 1999). Having regard to the fragility of the metals, these were divided into two groups:
    a. The most resistant were treated at temperatures of 750 degrees over a period of 24 hours;
    b. The weakest were treated with temperatures of 400 degrees over a period of 48 hours.

3. Consolidation – collage of fragments, reinforcing and filling the gaps and areas for bonding with folder epoxy and fiberglass. Finally were insulated with graphite and microcrystalline wax.

CONCLUSIONS

As a conclusion we can infer that this cavity has been occupied not only as mine extraction, but also as a possible shelter, even during the classical times.

Like we know from others roman mines it were worked by probable slaves and guarded by military, detected by the presence of archaeological arms. Some of these objects may not only be combat weapons, but hunt objects.

Inside the cave there were found several fireplaces and a big diversity of small, medium or large fauna with traits of debones and kitchen. Probably the room A was served to eat and being the military room, since it is also close to the entrance.

The humidity contexts were the artefacts were found lead us to exhume and apply methodologies from underwater

Figure 9 – Sword, in iron, double-edged, before (a) and after (b) the conservation treatment, from the raster C2, level 2

Figure 10 – Sword, in iron, before (a) and after (b) treatment of conservation, from raster C3, level 2

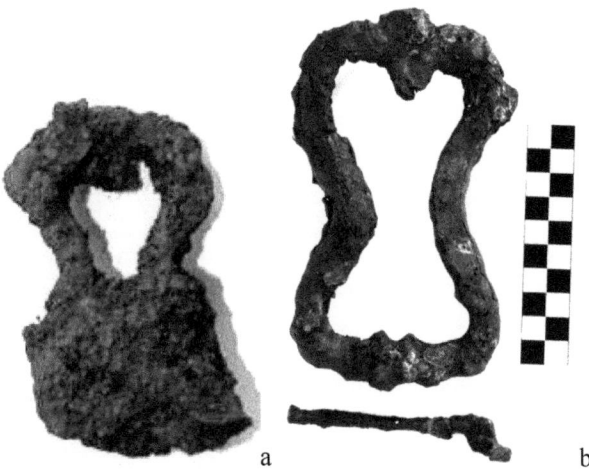

Figure 11 – Buckle, in iron, before (a) and after (b) the conservation treatment, coming from the raster B3, level 2

archaeology, mainly the metal artefacts that came to us, characterized in a way almost unrecognizable, with huge fouling and concretions.

The perception of these traces is relatively complex, were only a careful view of this type of deteriorations and

Figure 12 – Nozzle arms, in iron, before (a) and after (b) the intervention. we can verify the amount of concretions and encrustations before the intervention

pathologies could allow its proper collection, survey and preservation, as well as its correct referral to a specialist underwater laboratory for conservation. In this sense, we consider important to warn the scientific community about the importance of the humid caves, often relegated from the scope of underwater archeology and excavated by inexperienced eyes of these contexts. In fact, in all traces recorded by Santos Rocha, in the early twentieth century, from this place, we not known descriptions, nor iron artefacts archived at the Santos Rocha Museum (Figueirada Foz, Central Portugal), founded by us in a quite large number, even in the surface.

These objects, full of concretions and encrustations and a highly weakened state, confound us with his own soil and cave rocks and can be easily damaged by archaeological works. We know that when exposed to these environments its suffer from irreversible destruction complex. The choices are few, and basically, the conservative process is limited to the stabilization of the object, trying to preserve as much of the information possible. The survey should be performed by collecting soil together with the object on which it is located, involving in a gauze or in a film adhesive and placing it in an airtight and stable container. After this first cares made in field and the cleaning lab process, in the cases presented, since it are derived from a non-saline contexts, the tempering treatment proved to be a fast and effective method in the stabilization and elimination of chloride, allowing the subsequent consolidation and reconstruction of the objet and its further drawing and archaeological analysis.

References

ELIAZ, N. *et al.* (2002) – Characteristics of hydrogen embrittlement, stress corrosion cracking and tempered martensite embrittlement in high-strength steels. Pergamon, Engineering analysis 9. p. 167-184.

HAMILTON, D. (1999) – Methods of Conserving Archaeological Materialfrom Underwater Sites, Conservation Research Laboratory, Centre for Maritime Archaelogy and Conservation Texas A&M University.

ROCHA, A.S. (1853-1910) – Estação Luso-Romana da caverna do Bacelinho na serra de Alvaiázere, Porto: Imprensa Portuguesa. Portvgalia (digital version DVD). p. 137-139.

MATERIAL PRESERVATION VS MATERIAL CONSERVATION: ANALYSIS AND CONSERVATION OF ARCHEOLOGICAL MATERIAL OF THE SITE SC-NAUF-01, SANTA CATARINA, BRAZIL

Claudio MONTEIRO
Trás-os-Montes and Alto Douro University & Polytechnic Institute of Tomar
claudio.monteiro.cr@gmail.com

Deisi Scunderlick ELOY DE FARIAS
UNISUL / GRUPEP
deisiarqueologia@gmail.com

Alexandra FIGUEIREDO
Polytechnic Institute of Tomar
alexfiga@ipt.pt

Maria Matilde VILLEGAS JARAMILLO
UNISUL / GRUPEP
matildevillegas@terra.com.br

Marco Polo describes a bridge, stone by stone. – What is the Stone which maintain the bridge? Kublai Kan asks.
– The bridge is not maintained by this or that stone – Marco answers -, but by the arc line that they made. Kublai remains silent, thinking. After he adds:
– Why do you talk about stones to me? The only one that is important it is the arch.
Polo answers:
– Without stones there is no arch"
The invisible cities, Italo Calvino.

Abstract: *This work presents, in a brief form, the criteria used to analyse and conserve the archaeological material exhumed from the site SC-Naufragados[1]-01. This site is located in Baía Sul[2] in Florianópolis, Santa Catarina, Brazil, and it has been studied since 2010. From there it was withdrawn some archaeological material and their analysis had as aim identify the integrity degree of the pieces to, after, developing a suitable action plan to the conservation of the archaeological material. Some points lead this process: the conservation of archaeological material and its disclosure to the community and the development and adaptation of conservative technics and the analysis of the pieces in a historical perspective, where was highlighted, from a structured context, the reading of the artefacts, in this work understood as a representation of a historical period which involves the meeting between different cultures.*

Keywords: *Underwater Archaeology, Submerged Cultural Heritage, Conservation and Preservation*

Resumo: *Este artigo apresenta, de forma breve, os critérios adotados para a análise e conservação do material arqueológico exumado do sítio SC-Naufragados-01. Localizado na Baía Sul de Florianópolis, Santa Catarina, Brasil, que se encontra em estudo desde 2010. Nele registraram-se alguns materiais arqueológicos cuja análise permitiu identificar o grau de integridade das peças, para posteriormente, desenvolver um plano de ação adequado à conservação do material arqueológico. Dos pontos que nortearam este processo pautam-se: a conservação do material arqueológico e a sua extroversão para a comunidade, passando pelo desenvolvimento e adaptação de técnicas de conservação e a análise das peças numa perspectiva histórica, onde se destacou, a partir de um contexto estruturado, a leitura dos artefatos, aqui entendidos como a representação de um período histórico que envolveu o encontro entre culturas distintas.*

Palavras-chave: *Arqueologia Subaquática, Património Cultural Submerso, Conservação e Preservação*

INTRODUCTION

This work presents the methodology of analysis and conservation of stone and metal pieces exhumed from the archaeological site SC-NAUF-01, in southern Florianópolis, in Santa Catarina, Brazil, in 2010.

The main aim of this project presupposed an archaeological investigation based on theoretical parameters of the historic archaeology (Orser, 2000), with post-procedure bias (Hodder, 1994) which orient the hypothesis of the research in a wide area to be prospected and interpreted starting from comparison analyses by sampling (Gould, 2001; Fontenoy, 1998). The area studied presents several underwater and land archaeological sites previously identified (Juliani *et alli*,

---
[1] T.N.: Location name that means shipwrecked.
[2] T.N.: It is also a location name. Is located in South Bay.

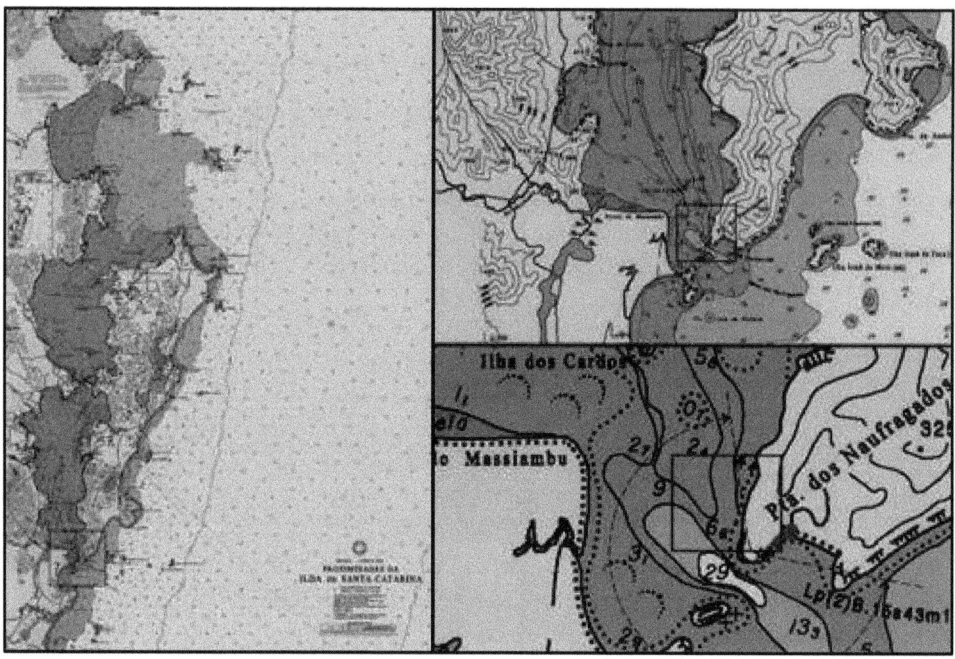

Figure 1 – Location of the archaeological site where treated materials were exhumed

2008). Some questions orient this research and they are going to be answered as the search progress and, above all, it is imperious know how the site was formed as well as the several evidences which compound it.

The archaeological station context has been evaluated by the group that is investigating the place. Some members of this group subscribe this article and they give relevance to structural and of the artefacts relations that compound the place as well as its preservation. The team appealed to designations purposed by Schiffer (1987) to understand post-depositional processes. This author distinguished them in cultural (Transformations – C) and natural (Transformations – N). Cultural Transformations involve deliberated or accidental human activities; Natural Transformations present natural causes that determine changes in the archaeological register. These distinctions are fundamentals to an adequate perception of human life and the past events, as in surface and posteriorly after submersion. These same procedures have several implications in the affection and preservation of the objects and they must be properly analysed during the intrusive archaeological processes. In this way, it is imperious the monitoring of experts in the conservation area to perform an efficient and safe extraction of the traces.

Starting from these theoretical and methodological presumptions and consciously that the historical objects and subjects emerge from discursive constructions (Rago, 2004), it was developed a small intrusive intervention. Some objects were emerged after these contextual register and the analysis of these conservation state. These objects were made in stone and metal and their preservation was in charge to GRUPEP-UNISUL.[3] The analysis was properly performed and their preservation processes was initiated in partnership with the Laboratory of Archaeology and Conservation of Underwater Heritage of Instituto Politécnico de Tomar.[4]

Altogether, there are four artefacts in stonework and some ballast stone, and a small fragment in metal.

The methodology used to clean the pieces in stone was based on Almeida (2005), Hamilton (1999) and Monteiro (2010; 2011). The aim of this analysis was identify the integrity degree of the pieces for, posteriorly, develop an adequate action plan to the conservation of the material.

Archaeological and historical data documented until this moment raise the hypotheses that several shipwreck occurred in that region, some of them was widely described in the chronicles of discovering and in another historical publications (Staden, 1974; Idem, 1992; Duran, 2008; Farias *et allii*, 2012). In a detailed documental research about the area where the site SC-NAUF-01 was observed, it has been registered the presence of a shipwreck from 16th Century. It belonged to a navy sailing toward the Strait of Magellan commanded by Diego Flores Valdés and Pedro Sarmiento de Gamboa (Boiteux, 1912 and 1919).

In fact, during the works of investigation, it was possible to produce a planialtimetric survey of the shipwreck. The plotting of traces allowed evaluating the current situation of the archaeological site. Current data were compared with historical data obtained and they point to a probable relation with reported data, what made this local a world important place. After the confirmation, it preservation will become indispensable.

---

[3] T.N.: Archaeological Research group – UNISUL, Universidade do Sul de Santa Catarina.

[4] T.N.: Polytechnic Institute of Tomar.

Frame 1 – Categories of artefacts identified in SC-NAUF-01

Categories of artefacts	Description
Category 1 – metal	Bronze cannon evidenced in the north side of the shipwreck; metal fragments on the ballast
Category 2 – artefacts in stonework	In the north side was evidenced a joint of four stones. They were three metres far from the cannon and it is possible they could be used as constructive marks and adornment to compose some kind of architectonic work.
Category 3 – Ballast stones	They compound the central part of the shipwreck.
Category 4 – Wood	Wooden plank measuring 100 x 30 centimetres and smaller in 0.50 x 0.10 centimetres.
Category 5 – Pottery	Pottery fragments.

In order to proceed a best identification of the historical and archaeological elements, it was essential develop a systematic excavation with detailed recognizing of the artefacts, as the case of the bronze cannon, whose date of foundry is 1563. Beyond this work, GRUPEP maintains a primary concern with exhaustive bibliographical research in an unceasing finding more documents and data which present reports about navigations and ship that sailed by Ocean Atlantic. These bibliographical research approach navigations toward Brazil Southern and Austral America, passing by Santa Catarina in several historic periods, particularly the documents referents to the shipwrecks in 16th Century, mainly those that occurred during the Iberian Union under government of D. Phillip II, wherewith was related this archaeological site.

BRIEF REPORT OF FIELD RESEARCH – INITIAL INTERPRETATIONS

The material analysed in this article is from archaeological site SC-NAUF-01 localized in Baía Sul Southern, near to Ponta dos Naufragados and Ilha do Papagaio Grande, in geographic coordinates 27°49 S / 048°34 W, in Florianópolis-SC. The research was performed in partnership of Barra Sul, a non-governmental Organization and GRUPEP-Archaeology/UNISUL. The Project was submitted to IPHAN[5] in 2010 and it previses the prospection of Baía Sul and the excavation of sites that were found within the area of the Project. After this stage, the Project became interdisciplinar and integrated experts from different areas. In 2011 was developed an agreement between UNISUL and Instituto Politécnico de Tomar, which involve the Laboratory of Archaeology and Conservation of Underwater Heritage in the treatment and analysis of recovered material, which resulted in this article.

Also around this time, it was performed the recognizing and inspection of the place with electronic prospections using Full Circle scanning sonar, Side Scan Sonar, echobathymeter and Global Positioning System equipment, metal detector and systematic diving in potential areas for archaeological sites indicated by these devices (Farias *et alli*, 2012).

Archaeological traces of SC-NAUF-01 are dispersed in an area of approximately twenty two metres of width by thirty metres of length atop of Sandy bottom covered by molluscs and algae. They are two kilometres from the shoreline; in this case, represented by Praia do Sonho;[6] one quilometre from Ponta dos Naufragados and three hundred metres from Praia do Defunto,[7] in Ilha de Santa Catarina.[8] This place is featured by the constant movement of sandbanks because of the ocean currents that crossed the canal (Farias *et alli*, 2012).

Over there was performed the following activities based on the methodologies purposed by Bass (1971); Blot (1998); Green (2004); Renfrew and Bahn (2007); Bowens (2009):

- Delimitation of the site with metal detector;
- Total scanning using direct prospecting technic;
- Definition of a point zero in the more elevated part of the site;
- Implantation of poitas[9] in order to demarcate the research area;
- Georeferencing of poitas by total GPS station;
- Photo mosaic of site;
- Mapping of ballast and dispersed traces;
- Analysis of preservation state of objects *in-situ*;
- Emersion of objects with potential to identify the shipwreck;
- Conservation of exhumed objects.

Through the prospection, it was possible identify five categories of artefacts presented in Frame 01 in the archaeological site area.

From the observed material, it was removed the four artefacts in stonework, a very rusty object in metal with concretions and some pieces of ballast.

THE CONSERVATION OF ARCHAEOLOGICAL MATERIAL

The preservation of an artefact must be a constant concern for the archaeologist who previses the research

---
[5] T.N: National Institute of Historical and Artistic Patrimony.
[6] T.N: Dream beach.
[7] T.N: Defunct beach.
[8] T.N: Santa Catarina Island, the Capital of the State.
[9] T.N.: Kind of weight used in substitution of anchor in small ship.

Figure 2 – Process of desalination

Figure 3 – a and b – Blazon of Lion and Castile with Portuguese symbol indicating the period of Iberian Union (1580-1640). We can easily observe two lions, one in the inferior right side and another in superior side and two towers on opposite corners of lions. They are crowned at the top. We can observe five Portuguese chines

field performing.[10] Then, we understand that every trace in an archaeological site, when it is removed from this environment, no matter whether is aquatic or in land, it can suffer some kind of deterioration. In the aquatic environment, the degradation parameters of the material are different from the processes in dry environment. The water is a crucial factor, but it can be also a misleading factor. An object that seems stay in good state, in fact, can stay in risk of total collapse. The only thing that maintains the material in its original form is the fact of its pores are filled with water and the loss of this element can lead to the destruction of its internal structure, provoking the deformation and total or partial disintegration of the object (Monteiro, in press). In this way, it is imperious a pre-evaluation of the materials *in situ* and a storage plan for the materials in medium and long term.

The material from SC-NAUF-01 passed by the follow stages: Storage in containers with water, desalination, and report in appropriate files, analysis and cleaning.

Identification, analysis and conservation of archaeological material

Four stonework was registered and they possibly were used as constructive or adornment elements (Fig. 1, 2 e 3). The general methodology of analysis used followed the precepts of Monteiro (2010, 2011, 2012) and involved, initially, the technical description of the pieces with manual testing of resistence, observation of rocklike mass by naked eye and binocular magnifying glass,

---

[10] In the sole paragraph of the Article 9 of the Ordinance 07/1988, the State delegates to the researcher total responsibility under the guard of the archaeological patrimony while the Project is in effect, besides, this ordinance provides, in the Article 5, item VII that must be exist a researcher institution responsible by the guard of the collection. In this Project, the responsible institution is the UNISUL through the GRUPEP-Archaeology.

Frame 2 – Description of stonework pieces

Description	Dimension				Material	Production techniques
	Width	Height	Depth	Diam		
Stone with blazon	74.5	93.0	22.0		Granite gneiss stone	Bas-relief sculpture
Triangular stone	74.0	108.0	16.5		Granite gneiss stone	Epigraphy
Sphere 1				24.5	Granite gneiss stone	Sculpture
Sphere 2				25.0	Granite gneiss stone	Sculpture

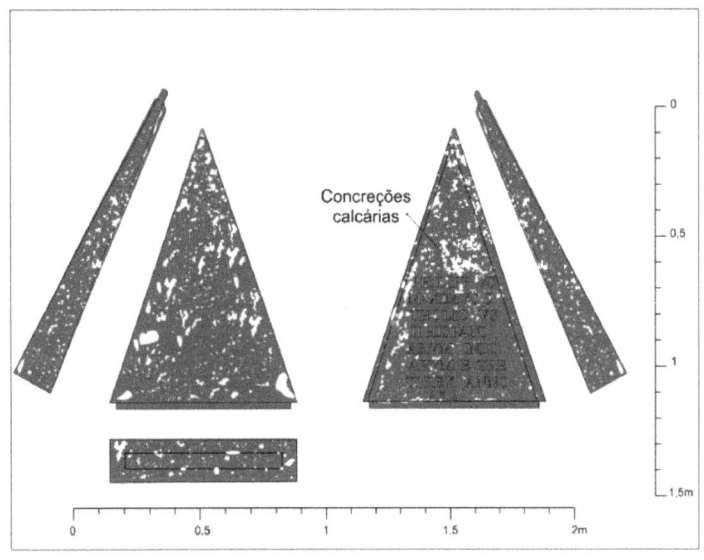

Figure 4 – Stone in triangular shape with bas-relief in Latin where we can read "PHILIPPVS MAXIMVS CATHOLICVS II HISPANIARVM INDIARVM ET REX ANNO 158.2" It is an allusion to King Phillip II

Figure 5 – Example of one of the spheres, possibly to compound an adornments architectonic work. There is a pyramidal engaging hole that is long-drawn until 1/3 of the piece

identification of concretion types by chemical tests and reporting on appropriate files of analysis involving attributes like: identification, proprieties, register, dimensions, historical and environmental context and conservation state (Frame 2).

After immersed, the material was storage in a polyurethane box, lined with high density EVA[11] and covered by a blanket to protect against eventual impacts. According to the analysis performed and the recognizing of pathologies in the material, we can summarize that the state of pieces found is satisfactory taking into account the rock hardness and the long period submersed in salt water. It was detected some chromatic changes, alveolarization, disintegration of cut material produced by concretions, incrustations and abrasion due to the environment changes wont to siltation caused by the movement of the tide.

The first process performed was desalination. The pieces passed by a process of changing of total water and constant monitoring of physical chemical parameters. Among them, we highlight the pH (hydrogen potential) which is used to express the intensity of acid or basic conditions in a solution and it is a way to express the concentration of hydrogen ion (Sawyer *et alli*, 1994 *apud* Farias, Correa 2006:11); and the electrical conductivity (CE) represented by the result measure of an electric force given, that is directly proportional to the quantity of

---
[11] T.N.: Vinyl polyacetate.

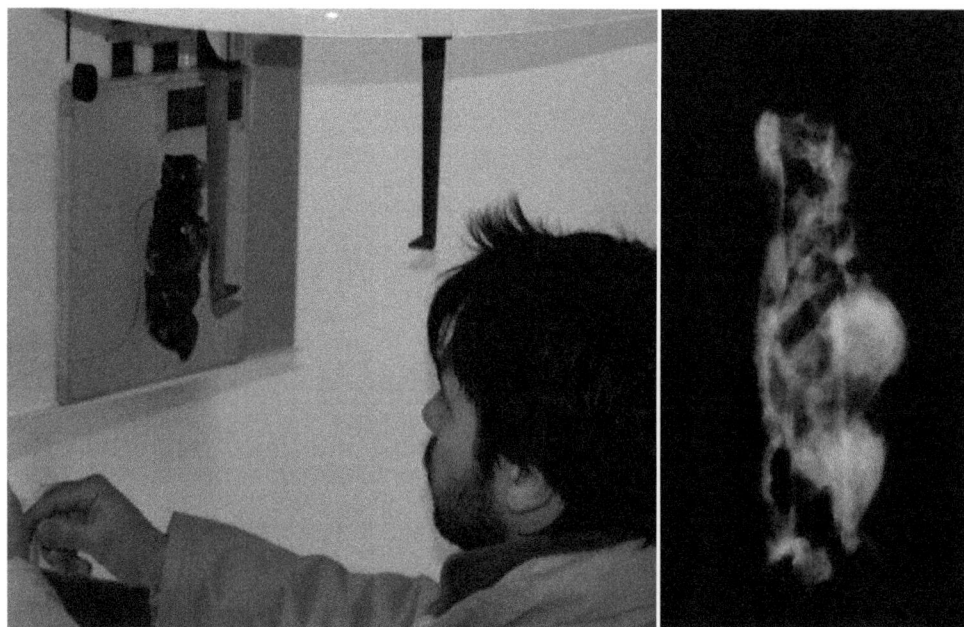

Figure 6 – The X-Ray allowed identify a fragment of a small iron rod of rectangular hollow section that possibly could be twisted by a rope, visible by traces of empty spaces left on the concretions

salts present in a solution. This process allows monitoring the presence of salts in the object by osmosis process. As the bathing are substituted, the salts are liberated to the solution until maintain in balance, producing variations in the conductivity of aqueous solution. The readings of conductivity, pH and temperature were performed with the devices *HI 98129 – pH/EC/TDS/Temperature with only one tester. Combo pH & EC. Hanna Instruments,* at the same hour of the day.

The cleaning of concretions will be performed after desalination. The aim is remove all substances that causes deterioration process in the pieces or contribute to it happened, like soluble salts, incrustations, vegetation infestation and animal waste; in this way it is possible protect the texture and appearance of the stone. The cleaning will be performed in controlled way, removing only the layers of particles necessaries to a good conservation of the stone, avoiding any possible aggression in the piece. The use of chemical products is restricted to the cases with proved necessity in order to avoid any change in the pieces (Almeida 2005:56).

Chemical cleaning will be performed systematically with embedded compresses in hydrochloric acid solution in 10%. The removal of concretions will allow the analysis of details not yet detected.

The metal object was submitted to tests of evaluation of metallic core. The results were negatives indicating total loss of metallic core. Based on this result, it was performed a X-Ray test in order to identify the object involved in the volume of concretions and products of oxidation.

The advanced state of oxidation made impossible the recovering of the object. We made the option for total removal of the humidity by Muffle in 102°C during 24 hours and posterior storage in a controlled environment.

About ballast stones, they were desalinated and storage in dry place.

FINAL REMARKS

The archaeological process of conservation continues in development. Next stages foresee a deepening in the study of research by intrusive or non-intrusive studies. The problem referred to the identification of the shipwreck needs a best inquest and it only will be possible by the continuing of researches that can identify new traces which corroborate the raised hypothesis of the "La Proveedora", ship belonged to the navy that followed to the Strait of Magellan and commanded by Diego Flores Valdés and Pedro Sarmiento de Gamboa, during the government of King D. Phillip II.

However, all this process only can be performed with an efficient plan of protection and preservation of the materials that would be recovered. With this aim, GRUPEP/UNISUL has been doing all the efforts to create a Laboratory of Conservation for submerged heritage and with the technical scientific support from Instituto Politécnico de Tomar (Portugal) and its Laboratory of Archaeology and Conservation of Underwater Heritage has been developing the competences to preserve recovered material from this archaeological site.

According to the dynamics and times inherent to the processes of underwater conservation, the objects recovered in 2011 are in treatment yet and we can forecast their exposition to the community in few time.

References

ALMEIDA, F.F.N. (2005) – Manual de Conservação de Cantarias. Brasília: IPHAN.

BASS, G.F. (1971) – Arqueologia Subaquática. 2ª edição, Lisboa, Editorial Verbo.

BLOT, J.Y. (1998) – From Peru to Portugal: field analysis of the last voyage of San Pedro de Alcantara. Bulletin of the Australian Institute for Maritime Archaeology, Fremantle, 22.

BOITEUX, L.A. (1912) – Notas para a História Catharinense. Florianópolis: Livraria Moderna.

BOITEUX, L.A. (1919) – História de Santa Catarina. São Paulo: Melhoramentos, 1919.

BOWENS, A. (2009) – Underwater Archaeology. The NAS Guide to Principles and Practices. The Nautical Archaeology Society.

DURAN, L.D. (2008) – A arqueologia marítima de um Bom Abrigo. São Paulo. Tese de Doutorado. MAE/USP.

FARIAS, D.S.E.; CORREA, G. (2006) – Projeto Resgate Barra Sul – Relatório Técnico Científico. Florianópolis: FAPESC.

FARIAS, D.S.E.; DEMATHÉ, A.; JARAMILLO, M.M.V.; GUIMARÃES, G.M. (2012) – *Projeto Resgate Barra Sul prospecção e pesquisa arqueológica sub-aquática, Baía sul de Florianópolis – Naufragados. Relatório Parcial de Pesquisa, Tubarão.*

FONTENOY, P. (1998) – A discussion of Maritime Archaeology. In: Babits, L; Tilburg, H.V. (eds). Maritime Archaeology. A reader of substantive and theoretical Contributions. New York, Plenum Press.

GREEN, J. (2004) – Maritime Archaeology. A technical handbook. Oxford, Academic.

GOULD, R. (2001) – Archaeology and the social history of ships. Cambridge, University Press.

HAMILTON, D.L. (1999) – Methods of conserving archaeological material from underwater sites. Texas: A&M University Press.

HODDER, I. (1994) – Reading the past Current approaches to intrepetation in Archaeology. Cambridge University Press.

JULIANI, L.M.J.O.; DURAN, L.D. (2008) – Contextualização de achado fortuito realizado durante etapa de monitoramento de instalação de cabos de travessia submarina da LT Biguaçu-Desterro (Sistema de reforço eletroenergético à ilha de Santa Catarina) município de Palhoça, SC. São Paulo. Relatório final.

MONTEIRO, C. (2010) – Relatório da Intervenção de Conservação de Cerâmica proveniente dos trabalhos de prospecção da Carta Arqueológica de Lagos 2010. Lagos, IGESPAR.

MONTEIRO, C. (2011) – Manual de Preservação de Espólio Submerso. Manual aplicado ao Curso de Pós-graduação de Arqueologia Subaquática, policopiado, Instituto Politécnico de Tomar, Tomar.

MONTEIRO, C. (in press) – The Study and Analysis of the Behaviour of Wet Archaeological Wood during the Drying Process: the Development of Drying Methods without the need of Consolidants or Plasticizers, BAR International Series, edited by Figueiredo, Alexandra, Callippo, Flavio and Rambeli, Gilson. *Proceedings of the XVI IUPPS World Congress (Florianopolis, 4-10 September 2011) / Actes du XVI Congrès Mondial UISPP (Florianópolis, 4-10 Septembre 2011), in press.*

ORSER, C.E. (2000) – Introducción a la arqueología histórica. Buenos Aires. AINA.

SCHIFFER, M.B. (1987) – Formation processes of the archaeological record. Albuquerque: University of New Mexico Press.

STADEN, H. (1992) – Viagens e aventuras no Brasil, Ed. Melhoramentos, 2ª. ed., 110 p.

STADEN, H. (1974) – Duas viagens ao Brasil. São Paulo/ Belo Horizonte: Edusp/Itatiaia.

STANIFORTH, Mark (2003) – Material Culture and Consumer Society. Dependent colonies in colonial Australia. New York, Kluwer Academic/Plenum Publishers, (The Plenum Series in Undewater Archaeology).

RAGO, M. (2004) – Foucault, História e Anarquismo. Rio de Janeiro, Achiamé.

RENFREW, C.; BAHN, P. (2007) – Arqueología, teorias, métodos y practica. 4ª ed. Madrid: Akal.

THE STUDY AND ANALYSIS OF THE BEHAVIOUR OF WET ARCHAEOLOGICAL WOOD DURING THE DRYING PROCESS: THE DEVELOPMENT OF DRYING METHODS WITHOUT THE NEED OF CONSOLIDANTS OR PLASTICIZERS

Cláudio MONTEIRO

Trás-os-Montes and Alto Douro University & Polytechnic Institute of Tomar
claudio.monteiro.cr@gmail.com

Abstract: *This presents the results of an ongoing research project on the preservation of water-saturated archaeological wood. The aim of this project is, firstly, to better understand the morphology and behaviour of wet archaeological wood when it is subjected to dehydration processes. Secondly, it aims to develop specific drying methods to control the damage caused by drying. To make this possible, a prototype of a chamber for environmental conversion has been developed in order to test drying methods used on materials recovered from water-soaked environments without, however, making use of / resorting to using consolidants.*

Keywords: *Conservation – Wood – Drying – Underwater archaeology – Organic matter*

Résumé: *Le but de cet article est de présenter un projet de recherche en cours sur la préservation de l'eau saturée en bois archéologique. Ce projet est destiné à comprendre la morphologie et le comportement des bois archéologiques humides lorsqu'ils sont soumis à des processus de déshydratation ainsi que de développer des méthodes spécifiques de séchage pour contrôler les dommages causés par le séchage. Pour ce faire, un prototype d'une chambre pour la conversion de l'environnement a été développé pour tester des méthodes de séchage utilisées sur les matériaux récupérés à partir des environnements d'eau sans la nécessité d'utiliser des agents de consolidation.*

Mots-clés: *Conservation – Bois – Sechage – Archéologie sous-marine – Organique*

RESEARCH AIMS

This research project focuses on the conservation of wet archaeological wood.

Our aim is to study the behaviour of wet degraded wood during the drying process and to develop methods which will allow for the dehydration of wood without resorting to the addition of consolidants or filling resins. For this purpose we have developed a new method that will allow for the regeneration of wood tissues, unlike what occurs in traditional consolidation processes.

INTRODUCTION

Ever since work on the conservation of underwater archaeological materials began, conservators have attempted to stabilise and to dry wood artefacts and at the same time causing the least amount of damage. The conservation of organic materials, and particularly wood, has proved to be a real scientific challenge, although many problems have already been solved as a result of the advances in conservation science. However, all the methods developed so far have revealed some fundamental drawbacks, either because they are too aggressive to be used on artefacts or because of the consequences they will have or might have in the long term. What is more, many projects are not feasible because of the size of the artefacts or because of the exorbitant cost of treatments.

The aim of this paper is to make better known the preliminary results of an ongoing research project on a new approach to the conservation of archaeological wood.

Wood is a natural polymer with unique properties and for that it should be studied in-depth, examined and very well understood. Its behaviour and its reactions in the face of external stimuli (inner property of wood) suggest that it can be induced to attain a certain altered state when external stimuli are oriented in a different direction. This treatment strategy rests on the presupposition that wood should be treated as a polymer and not with polymers.

THE CONSERVATION OF SATURATED ARCHAEOLOGICAL WOOD

Over the years, significant progress has been made in the technologies behind the conservation of saturated archaeological wood. First there were developed the drying methods with natural solvents and oils, then new advantages led to the rosin method and to the PEG resins (Astrup 1994; Hamilton 1999; Olvera 2001) after appeared the lyophilisation (Hamilton 1999; Schindelholz 2007), more recently was adapted the process of drying with supercritical fluids (Teshirogi 2001; Lumia *et al.*, 2003; Schindelholz 2007) and the use of silicon oils (Hamilton 1999; Smith 2003).

However, although the results from these technologies are satisfactory and acceptable, they are not without their disadvantages and they also have side effects on the artefacts treated. Logistics and financial constraints are crucial issues as the conservation of these materials involves extremely high, and sometimes the costs are exorbitant. Size is also a constraint that remains to be overcome. Even the case of the Swedish ship Vasa is far from being a success case (Baglioni *et al.*, 2006). Preservation *in situ* has been a sensible solution and we believe it is an idea to retain and further develop (Lillie and Smith 2009).

The PEG resins it is the most common method. This process presents one major drawback, that is the fact that the object cannot be brought back to its original size (Olvera 2001), which consequently prevents any reconstruction of composite objects; If we accept the assumption that these are very aggressive chemical treatments, then the fact that they cause significant changes in the artefacts would be another drawback (Baglioni *et al.*, 2006).

Lyophilisation is an attractive method but it does not dispense of the use of PEG (Jesen 2002). Its application to large-size artefacts is difficult because the use of an air-tight chamber capable of producing very negative temperatures and control pressures becomes progressively more difficult as the size of the artefact increases, and this makes this sort of equipment financially prohibitive.

Even though it has revealed some very interesting results (Hamilton 1999; Smith 2003), the use of drying with silicon oils is compromised when it comes to large-size artefacts, this on account of the logistics, the products and the equipment involved in the process.

Although it has also provided some very good results (Teshirogi 2001; Schindelholz 2007), drying with supercritical fluid has the drawbacks of requiring solvents and of being difficult to use in large-scale treatments. The reasons are the same as for the ones described for lyophilisation, although, in this case, these do not have to do with low temperatures, but rather with the difficulty of controlling pressure in large chambers.

TREATMENT IN ENVIRONMENTAL CONVERSION CHAMBER

This method was designed so as to overcome some of the disadvantages of the existing processes. For this purpose, a chamber has been built which has special characteristics that induce certain inputs into environmental control. The aim of this method is to reconditioning existing wood tissues by means of a specific drying program. The expected result is a dried wood with a natural look and resistance.

In order to understand this process, we must first understand wood behaviour. The wood when immersed in alkaline or acidic water, suffers a slow hydrolysis (Klock 2005) in which the final result is the dispersion of the monomers that forming the cellulose, hemicellulose and lignin. Although, this turns out to be a very slow process in the archaeological degradations contexts, being overtaken by bacterial deterioration which consumes the polymers.

Of the three wood polymers, lignin is the one that preserves best and it is, in part, because of this that wood artefacts do not disintegrate. However, during the drying process the loss of cellulose and hemicellulose content in the cell walls causes, not only the loss of resistance in the walls, but also an imbalance of stress forces within the wood tissues. This situation becomes critical when drying is rapid because it causes an imbalance in moisture gradients and promotes an anisotropic behaviour in wood. Our main concern has been, therefore, to understand how this can be overcome. We have focused on creating an artificial environment that promotes controlled, balanced drying, and which eliminates all the stresses caused by asymmetrical dehydration and allows wood to maintain appropriate balance gradients. Another significant factor to be taken into account is the drying rate: this will be the lower, whenever tissues are in a more fragile state. Low temperatures in this case are extremely important because the mechanical resistance of wood increases and, consequently, its resistance to collapsing. This means that the lower the temperature, the bigger the drying rate can be.

Drying is thus carried out by taking into account the properties of the wood and its moisture content and level of degradation, each time using a specific dry programme adapted to each individual case. In our chamber have been tested some theoretical drying models to try to figure what really happens in the reality to the woods elements.

The first program tested was a binary one which is carried out over two phases. An initial phase conducted by drying by evaporation and another one made by a thermal conduction applied alternately (figure 1). Theoretically, this process allows a slow and gradual dehydration interspersed with balanced thresholds of moisture gradients. Together with heat treatment, this process allows for the re-polymerisation of cellulose, hemicellulose and lignin without changing the shape and dimensions of form, thereby permitting their reconstruction, glueing and assemblage.

This programme permits the reduction of stresses created by the differences in moisture gradients inside the wood, thus preventing it from collapsing or cracking. On the other hand, the low drying rate and the balance thresholds offset the capillary stress exerted by water, thus preventing cells from collapsing during drying. Another advantage of this process is that it permits the correction of deformations caused by track twists (figure 2 and 3). These deformations have been able to be corrected in primary tests.

In the treatment plans carried out so far, some side effects continue to be observed; this can be accounted by the

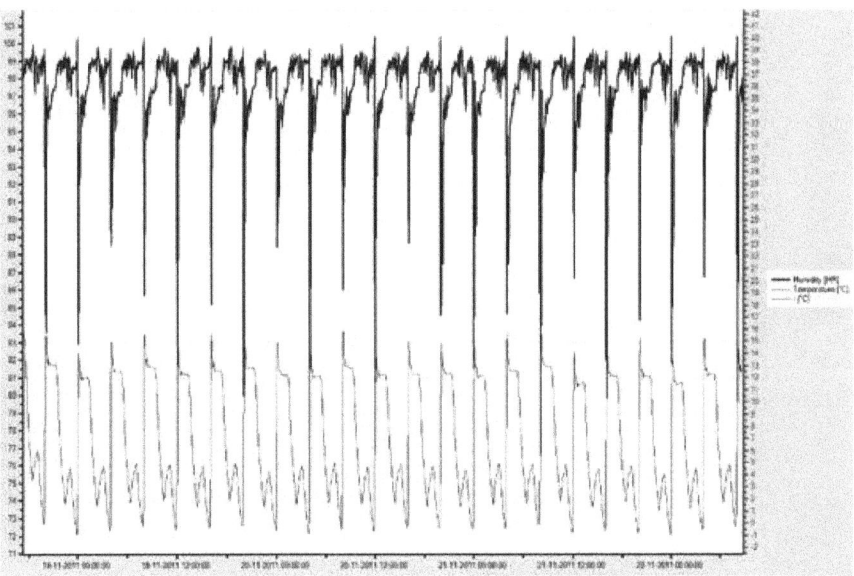

Figure 1 – Drying program in sample A2

Figure 2 – Wood before treatment[1]

Figure 3 – Wood after treatment

difficulty that the prototype has in meeting the requirements of the theoretical model, in particular the rigor of the values of humidity and temperature.

Because of a lack of funding for this project, the environmental conversion chamber is very rudimentary, which makes it difficult to use more complex drying programmes, as well as to obtain better more reliable data.

SAMPLES BEING HANDLED

Test treatments have been used on two types of samples:

a. Lab-degraded samples:

Pinus Pinaster samples were degraded in an alkaline solution of sodium hydroxide, heated at 60°C for 48 hours and then left in the solution for 5 months.

---

[1] Wood degraded in sodium hydroxide at 60°C.

b. Archaeological samples:

The samples are from the Portuguese sites Ria de Aveiro A and Ria de Aveiro F and are courtesy of DANS (Nautical and Underwater Archaeology Division) of IGESPAR (Institute for the Management of Architectural and Archaeological Heritage).

The wood samples tested so far are *Pinus Pinaster* and *Betula Alba* (although identification of the latter is still in doubt because of its advanced state of decay).

This paper will focus primarily on the treatment carried out on a *Betula Alba* sample with an estimated moisture content of about 667.7%. It is a Class 1 in terms of decay. Its deterioration is generalized; it looks spongy and has been subjected to the attacks of soft-rot fungi.

Its condition is extremely fragile and when it is dried in the air, such as it was done in the initial test, it reaches a critical rate of deformation and becomes simply unrecognisable.

DISCUSSION OF THE RESULTS

Despite the fact that these were test conditions and even though this was our first test, we suggest that these are very promising results, even if they are not completely satisfactory in relation to the expected outcomes.

The information data stemming from these works is of considerable interest to the scientific community:

- First, wood has the capacity to reconditioning itself by recovering its mechanical resistance. This is the result of dehydration: when wood dries, the natural polymers in the wood tissues crystallise and recover its physical properties. In fact, the hardness observed in the sample after it has been dried was quite impressive. While in

Figure 4 – A1 Before   *Figure 5 – A1 After*

Figure 6 – A2 Before   *Figure 7 – A2 After*

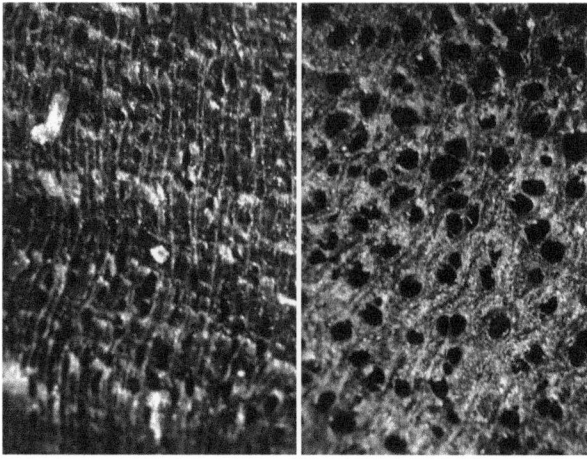

Figure 8 – A1 After being dried 40x   *Figure 9 – A2 After being dried 40x*

the case of the air-dried sample (which we shall refer to as A1 – figure 4 and 5) the hardness could have been caused by compression resulting from cells collapsing, in the case of the chamber-dried sample (which we shall refer to as A2 – figure 6 and 7) this could not have applied as the pores of medium-size vessels and cells remained unchanged.

- Another relevant detail has to do with the fragmentation of the wood after drying up. Differently from sample A2, despite its hardness sample A1-broke up easily in the axial direction. This could be on account of the extreme fragility of the cell walls given that in sample A1 these are very fragmented as a result of their collapse. Fragmentation seems to occur at the folding points in the cell walls and the deformation stress causes the disruption of fibres in the cell wall tissues (figure 8). In sample A2, the fact that wall tissue seems to have remained intact could be explain of the increased cohesion of the cells (figure 9).

- Regarding sample deformation, there was a significant increase in air drying, A1 took 6 days to dry in a winter environment at temperatures between 12 and 17 degrees Celsius and a R.H. of about 50% and 70%. The end result was a piece of wood which was unrecognisable on account of its high deformation. The A2 sample showed only a slight deformation when compared to A1. The overall shape of the sample was maintained; however, it did not attain the level of exact shape that was desired. It is worth noting that, when analysed under a microscope, the vessels and cells in the wood tissue appear to be intact and to have been preserved. So far we have not yet been able to examine the samples under the electronic microscope, and therefore cannot yet draw any conclusions about the behaviour of small-diameter cells.

- The deformation of sample A2 suggests that part of the fibres and fibro-tracheids collapsed and that this was the cause of the deformation. Considering that the diameters of these cells are significantly smaller than the vessels and tracheids, the forces resulting from capillary tension are also significantly greater. Theoretically, this problem could be solved through a more rigorous programme involving the reduction of temperature range and humidity.

- When we turn to contraction rate, we see that the sample A1 is about 70% of its initial volume; because of the deformation it is not possible to determine shrinkage in each of the sections. Sample A2 shows a radial shrinkage of about 22% and a tangential shrinkage of about 33%. In the axial direction no change was observed. These values are above the range of those considered acceptable, but these values may be improved if the collapse of smaller cells which leads to an increase in volume is prevented.

- The relationship between the fibre saturation point (FSP) and wood shrinkage is of little consequence when applied to water-saturated, degraded wood. In cases like these there is no matching pattern and neither is it possible to establish a fixed threshold. This relationship is also very difficult to establish in very degraded woods because of the severe deformation caused by collapsing. *Pinus Pinaster* samples which were degraded in the laboratory with a moisture content of 240% revealed an FSP of about 80%, which contrasts with the 30% normally seen in fresh young wood. These values should, in part, come as no surprise, given that FSP in green wood's is not the saturation point of fibres, but is, instead, partial, in the sense that fibres might not be at their maximum saturation capacity, unlike what happens with wood from underwater settings. These studies need to be further refined.

- Another point to bear in mind when comparing sample A1 and A2 is that A2 shows some internal cracks

Figure 10 – B1 Before starting process

Figure 11 – B1 During process

Figure 12 – B1 Final Phase of process

Figure 13 – B2 Before starting process

Figure 14 – B2 During process

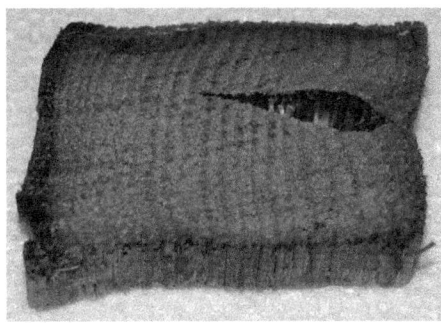

Figure 15 – B2 Final Phase of process

(figures 13, 14 and 15) which suggests that the moisture gradients were not properly balanced and caused inner stresses. On the other hand, internal cracking was observed in A1 (*figures 10, 11 and 12*). This type of anomaly is on account of the fact that the drying technique used in A2 eliminates drying through capillary flow, i.e. the cross-section is insulated so as not to allow water flow in the axial direction, forcing the water to flow through pores and cell walls. Understanding this behaviour is crucial if anisotropy in wood is to be reduced during the drying process because the relationship between tangential and radial drying is much more balanced than the relationship that these two have with axial drying. The capillary flow is tens or even hundreds of times faster, because the obstacles that need to be overcome by the water are substantially smaller in the longitudinal direction. For that reason it appears that the control of moisture gradients is easier with this method.

In order to understand this drying dynamic, two samples were tested in a drying oven at 60ºC, one under free drying conditions (B1) and the other with insulated tops (B2). B1 did not suffer greater shrinkage than B2, but no internal cracking was observed.

Although also deformed, B2 had a smaller contraction rate which contributed to a smaller deformation. However, there was the formation of a huge crack which started in the external surface and spread inside, finally closing in the peripheral area. This occurred because regular drying takes place from outside to inside. When the outer area dries, the inner area is still damp and swollen. Because it loses water much faster, the shrinking process starts more quickly in the external area. Differences in volume between these two areas cause cell disruption and the resultant internal and external cracking (Hoadley 1999).

In contrast to this, the drying in B1 was much faster and homogeneous because of the small axial length of the sample. However, the high drying rate caused the significant collapse of cells.

This trial experiment intended to demonstrate the water diffusion dynamics in wood during the drying process. In a real situation, i.e. with a bigger specimen, the two drying types (B1 and B2) actually / would actually / may coexist, causing asymmetrical drying. For that reason, top insulation becomes all the more important, the greater the fragility of wood.

CONCLUSIONS

The results obtained so far revealed themselves to be promising and have opened the avenues for advances in further research. If this method proves to be viable, it will become invaluable in the preservation of artefacts from our underwater heritage in that it will reduce costs and the associated logistical problems while, at the same time, contributing to a more ecological and stable treatment of archaeological objects. In addition, treatment time could be significantly reduced given that has been predicted that 3 cm-thick wood specimens samples, no matter what their length is, can be treated in less than 6 months.

The size of objects should not be an obstacle, and the greatest expenditure will be in the construction of the environmental conversion chamber, although the greater its use, the more profitable it will be. The advantage of this chamber is that it can be built in large sizes, thus allowing for the treatment of several objects at any one time.

The fact that one of our objectives is not to use consolidants does not mean that a consolidant cannot be used in extreme situations. However, concentrations of these consolidants may be much smaller than those used to date.

We believe that this method, if further improved, will be very effective in wood with a moisture content of up to 400%.

References

ASTRUP, E.E. (1994) – A Medieval Log House in Oslo – Conservation of Waterlogged Softwoods with Polyethylene Glycol. Proceedings of the 5th ICOM Group on Wet Organic Archaeological Materials Conference, Portland, Maine. 16-2- August 1993. p. 41-50.

BAGLIONI, Michele; POGGI, Giovanna (2006) – Degrado e Conservazione del Legno del Vascello Vasa: Le Nuove Frontiere Della Chimica Per la Conservazione della nave da Guerra piú Imponente della Flotta Svedese del XVII Secolo, Rivista On line Associazione Italiana Esperti in Diagnostica Applicata ai Beni Culturali Numero 1 I Semestre.

HAMILTON, Donny L. (1999) – Methods of conserving Archaeological Material from Underwater Sites, Nautical Archaeological Program, Department of Anthropology, Texas A&M University Press, College Station.

HOADLEY, Bruce R. (1997) – Understanding Wood, A Craftsman's guide to wood technology, Taunton Press, Inc. U.S.A.

JESEN, Poul; JORGENSEN, Grethe; SCHNELL, Ulrich (2002) – Dynamic LV-SEM Analyses of Freeze Drying Processes for Waterlogged Wood, *Proceedings of the 8th ICOM Group on Wet Organic Archaeological Materials Conference, Stockholm, 11-15 June 2001.* p. 319-333.

KLOCK, Umberto; MUNIZ, Graciela; HERNANDEZ, José; ANDRADE, Alan (2005) – Química da madeira, 3ª edição, Universidade Federal do Paraná, Setor de Ciências Agrárias, Departamento de Engenharia e Tecnologia Florestal, Brasil.

LILLIE, Malcolm; SMITH, Robert (2009) – International Literature Review: *In Situ* Preservation of Organic Archaeological Remains, English Heritage, Wetland Archaeology & Environments Research Centre.

LUMIA, G.; PERRE, Ch.; SCHRIVE, L.; BARTH, F.; CHAUMAT, G.; ARACIL, J.M. (2003) – Supercritical CO2 is a Tool For Natural Material Treatments, 6th International Symposium on Supercritical Fluids, ISASF, 28 to 30 April, Versailles, France.

OLVERA, Alejandra Alonso; REYES, Ma. Teresa Tzompantzi; ANAYA, Demetrio Mendoza (2001) – Conservación de Maderas Arquológicas Húmedas: Perpectiva actual y retos para el Futuro en México, Conserva Nº 5. p. 57-79.

SHINDELHOLZ, Eric (2007) – An Evaluation of Supercritical and PEG/Freeze Drying of Waterlogged Archaeological Wood, National Center for Preservation Technology and Training Grant.

SMITH, C. Wayne (2003) – Archaeological Conservation Using Polymers, Practical Applications for Organic Artifact Stabilization, Texas A&M University Press, College Station.

TESHIROGI, Miho; TAHATA, Eiichiro; KIKUCHI, Mikio; HNOMATA, Hiroshi; KOHDZUMA, Yohsei; KOEZUKA, Takayasu; SAWADA, Masaaki (2001) – Conservation Treatment of Water-logged Wood Whid Supercritical Carbon Dioxide, *Proceedings of the 8th ICOM Group on Wet Organic Archaeological Materials Conference, Stockholm, 11-15 June 2001* p. 371-376.

www.ingramcontent.com/pod-product-compliance
Ingram Content Group UK Ltd.
Pitfield, Milton Keynes, MK11 3LW, UK
UKHW061213180426
11947UKWH00029B/2036